THE GODFREY DIARY

The Field Diary of

LT. EDWARD SETTLE GODFREY

Commanding Co. K, 7th Cavalry Regiment under

Lt. Colonel George Armstrong Custer

in the

Battle of the Little Bighorn

May 17, 1876 to September 24, 1876.

PLUS

Godfrey's famous 1892 *Century Magazine* article

Discover more lost Custer books at BIG BYTE BOOKS

Contents

PUBLISHER'S NOTES

Edward Settle Godfrey (1843–1932) is an obscure figure in American history and cannot even be said to be forgotten by most, as they would never have paid attention to the name. Yet he was at the center of one of history's most written-about events: the Battle of the Little Bighorn. To Little Bighorn scholars and students, Godfrey is a familiar man. He was one of the soldiers who testified in 1879 at the Reno Court of Inquiry.

Godfrey at the time of the battle (June 1876) was 1st Lieutenant commanding Company K of the 7th Cavalry, under the leadership of Lieutenant-Colonel (Brevet General) George Armstrong Custer. Company K was under the battalion leadership of Captain (Brevet Colonel) Frederick W. Benteen, who remained a friend of Godfrey's for many years after their service together in the 7th.

Godfrey is important to the study of the Bighorn battle for various reasons, not least of which is the fact that he, like many soldiers, kept a diary on the 1876 Yellowstone Expedition.

He was also involved in three events of note from June 25th, the start of the battle, to June 28th, when the columns left the battle site for the mouth of the Little Bighorn and the steamer *Far West*.

First, when Captain Thomas Weir made his unauthorized advance on the afternoon of June 25th from what later became the Reno-Benteen Defense site, north along Sharpshooter Ridge to what is now called Weir Point, Godfrey was not far behind, as was most of the Reno command. They soon found themselves in a hasty retreat to a defensive position in a shallow swale as attacking warriors approached. Godfrey commanded the skirmish line thrown out to cover the retreat.

Godfrey states that he did this on his own initiative but Benteen later wrote that he had ordered Godfrey to throw out the line and to "hold it at all hazards." A minor point, but the fact is, all but one man made it to the defense area alive. Vincent Charley was shot in the hip and told to hide until they could come back for him. He was killed and recent archaeology has likely identified his remains (see *Uncovering History*, Scott, 2013). Twice during this retreat, Godfrey had to calm his men, reform his line, and was obviously an effective field officer.

Second, Godfrey had a conversation with Captain Weir on the night of 25 June (after the Indians had stopped firing on the

6

soldiers). Weir asked Godfrey, "If there should be a conflict of judgment between Reno and Benteen as to what we should do, whose orders would you obey?" Godfrey states that without hesitation, he replied, "Benteen's." The implication was that Weir agreed with Godfrey, regardless of the fact that this would be mutinous, as Reno was the ranking officer.

In fact, many of the men at the battle attributed their survival to the coolness and courage of Frederick Benteen.

Third, Godfrey had a conversation with Benteen on the afternoon of the 27th. The Indians had vacated the Little Bighorn valley, the relief column had arrived, and Benteen's troops were ordered to go to the Custer battlefield to identify the dead.

On the way there, Godfrey alluded to Major Reno's lack of leadership over the past days. Benteen apparently replied, "God [Godfrey's nickname], I could tell you things that would curl your hair." Just then someone came up and it would be years before Godfrey could get Benteen to reluctantly reveal what he'd been about to say. He was going to say that Reno had proposed on the night of the 25th to evacuate the area, leaving those wounded who could not ride behind to certain death. Benteen told Reno he could not do that. Apparently Benteen told this story to Lieutenant Charles Varnum and others as well.

In the diary, Godfrey mentions the already-burgeoning controversy over the battle appearing in the newspapers before the 7th even got back to Fort Lincoln in September. And it is remarkable how quickly things seemed to return to the normal cares of camp life, just days after the carnage at LBH.

Godfrey had served in the Civil War, later attending West Point on the strength of his performance in the field. He won a Medal of Honor for his actions at the Battle of Bear Paw Mountain and later fought in Cuba. He retired a Brevet Brigadier General.

The diary is made up of two small pocket notebooks, written in pencil—rough field notes, unrevised. They reside in the Library of Congress.

THE *CENTURY MAGAZINE* ARTICLE

In 1892, Edward Godfrey wrote a highly influential article for *Century Illustrated Magazine*. The article had wide circulation and has been cited by Custer scholars ever since. It makes fascinating reading, not only for what Godfrey says about the Battle of the Little

Bighorn, but for what he doesn't say. Marcus Reno was dead by 1892 but many of the principal actors were still on the stage and Godfrey was still an army man—a 7th Cavalry one at that.

Godfrey had begun to be more sympathetic to Custer's actions at the battle. This was cause for a cleavage with his friend Benteen (whose antipathy to Custer predated the battle and remained to his death), although the two men corresponded in a friendly manner until Benteen's death.

Reading between the lines of Godfrey's article, you get a sense of his discontent with Reno and questions about the behavior of others at the Custer battle. Coupled with the diary we have here two of the most important "Custer" documents found in the bibliography of every serious Custer book.

Godfrey suspected that Reno had been drinking on the day of the battle. One soldier later reported seeing Reno taking hits from a flask *during the charge in the valley*! (It's hard to imagine noticing something like this during a cavalry charge, not to mention doing it.) Reno years later told a friend that his behavior at the Little Bighorn was due to drink. And it certainly is no secret that drink was the undoing of Reno's subsequent career.

As for Godfrey, he became the most familiar expert on the battle during his lifetime. He participated in a number of Little Bighorn reunion activities, including attending the 50th anniversary of the battle at the battleground.

Aside from the great value the article has for Little Bighorn scholars and enthusiasts, it also has wonderful details about cavalry life during a march. And it goes into more detail regarding some of the incidents mentioned in the diary, *e.g.*, Custer's mood and demeanor on the march.

Anyone with an interest in the Battle of the Little Bighorn, its controversy, its flamboyant leader, or the life of the average soldiers who fought and died there, will find something to fascinate them in Edward Settle Godfrey's documents. We are most fortunate that such men took the time to record their impressions and knew the value of keeping them long after the events had passed.

THE FIRST DIARY

Note: The original diary can be difficult to read due to Godfrey's inconsistent punctuation and capitalization. It has been edited for readability while retaining the idiosyncrasies that characterize the diary. That said, Godfrey's grammar and spelling exceeds in accuracy that of many of his contemporaries. Words and sentences that are struck out or underlined are from the original.

NOTES

Godfrey scribbled a few interesting notes in the beginning of the first pocket diary prior to the chronology, some of which are too faded to decipher. He notes two checks drawn on the 1st National Bank, as well as some small deposits. In very faded pencil, it appears he noted small deposits for shoemaker Thomas Murphy (1853–1909), a private in his company. These were probably deposits to the paymaster. He wrote May 17, the date they left Fort Lincoln, at the top of the page.

He left a page blank and then wrote:

Co. Memorandum

No [?] amount of transportation from 757 [?] comd. to Cin. O[hio].

Penwell [Company K trumpeter]

A small "C" trumpet at music store C[?] St near Royal N.C. ($2.50)

Deposit with p.m. [paymaster] $40.10 effects of [?] Young late private Co. K 7th Cav.

He then provides a list of incidentals but doesn't note whether these are purchases or just items packed. The legible items include cups, dishes, toothpicks, quills, paper, a soup tureen, a milk pitcher, a coffee mill, a half dozen "breakfast plates," and a half dozen saucers.

On the final page before the chronology begins, he wrote "Penwell $1.00" at the top and then there are a few columns of addition.

At the top of the beginning page of the chronology, he wrote: N.F. [North Fork] of Heart River to Camp on <u>Creek</u> 19 ¾ Crossed—our camp beside wood, water. 15

THE START

May 17 1876.

Our Route from Lincoln[1] was over the usual route in a westerly direction to the crossing of [18]73 and [18]74, where we encamped on E side. Good camp, wood & water. p.m. p[ai]d. troops. We found a bad crossing of Heart River (12 miles) on the 18th but made only about 10 miles & camped near Sweet briar [Creek]. No wood within ½ mile.

19th.—Kept on S. side of Sweet Briar; roads very heavy & camped on br[anch] of Mud (?) [question mark in original]. Roads heavy & just as we were going to camp, hailstorm. Some wagons did not get in till next am. nowd, nowat [no wood, no water].

20th. Did not leave camp till late roads still heavy but improving. Camp near forks of some stream, perhaps br. of Muddy (?); good grass, no wood.

21st. Camped on br. of mudy [sic] water in holes; Wood some distance off on hills. Had Heart Butte & Twin Buttes in view nearly all day. Very good march, roads improving.

22nd. Camped Br[anch of] Knife River where we camped in '73 (opposite). Six miles from Young Man's Butte.[2]

23rd. Marched to Y. M. Buttes—wood and water.

24. Marched to forks of Heart River, 19 miles, good camp.

25. X [crossed] N.F. Heart River & marched between forks & camped on branch of South Fork.

26. Camped on a Br. of Heart River.

---

[1] Fort Abraham Lincoln (1872–1891) was abandoned and disassembled by locals for materials. Portions have since been restored, including a replica of the house where the Custers lived.
[2] Near present Hebron, ND.

May 27. Left camp on branch of Heart River and went in southerly direction and struck the Bad Lands of the Little Mo. [Missouri River], near Genl Stanley's trail [of 1873], but through some oversight we crossed the trail & went two miles before the error was discovered. After waiting for about two hours, scouts were sent back to see if we had crossed it and in a short time they returned with the tidings that they had found it.[3] We went down Davis Creek and camped about 2 miles from the entrance to the Bad Lands.

Got a mail this A. M.—two letters from my darlings. All well. Mary[4] <u>struck</u> for higher wages.

May 28. Was Rear Guard today, but all the left flank Cos. were in the Rear too. The train moved briskly for about three miles, and then work began on the crossings [bridges] of the creek which runs from the Bluffs on one side to bluffs on the other; some seven (7) had to be constructed and then we went into camp. The 4th Battalion (Cos. G, K and M) had to go out & construct two (2) more crossings. We made them in about two hours. Maguire[5] superintended one and I the other. Spring near 8th crossing. Distance marched, 4 ½ miles. Made camp at 12.30. Wrote to Mary expecting the mail to go out.

May 29th. Little Mo. Was in the advance today and had to build several crossings but had less work than we anticipated and got to the Little Mo. at 9:30. The wagon train did not come in till an hour later. My Company was on picket duty & I had to go on a high Butte to post them. I was very tired, but found my tent occupied by poker players. I waited until 11 p.m. and told them they would have to <u>git</u> and they <u>got</u>. We marched today 6 ¾ miles.

---

[3] This navigation error may be the one referred to in *Custer's Scouts at the Little Bighorn: The Arikara Narrative* (2014, BIG BYTE BOOKS). Custer had ridden far ahead and his African American scout, Isaiah Dorman, had led the columns down the wrong fork in the road. The Arikara's told of seeing Dorman later on his knees in front of an angry Custer, begging for forgiveness.

[4] Mary Jane Pocock (1845–1883), Godfrey's first wife.

[5] Edward Maguire was also the engineer detailed by General Terry to map the Custer battlefield before the forces departed the Little Bighorn site on 28 June, 1876.

May 30. Genl Custer with Cos C, D, F, & M went on a scout up the Little Mo. about 20 miles & returned without having seen any signs of Indians. Played cribbage with McIntosh[6] and Jack Sturgis[7] and wrote to Mamma.[8] Rained in the evening.

May 31st. Didn't break camp today till 8 a.m. on account of tentage being wet. We crossed the Little Mo. without difficulty, and the train moved up the gorge, which is about 2 miles long, very easily, one wagon upset. We were on the left flank of the train and moved along without any trouble. I think a good road could be made down the creek which empties above the gorge and in case of an attack the train could be defended more easily. The valley seems like a smooth one. However, that can only be determined by an examination. We marched directly to the east foot of Sentinel Butte and then struck down a divide toward a branch of Anderson's Creek. The route was very circuitous and took us a number of miles out of our way. We were on Whistler's Trail. The best way I think would be to keep on the north side of both Sentinel Buttes. There is plenty of wood, water is doubtful except after a rain. Finished my letter to Mamma and wrote to Guysie[9] and put them in the mail. Rained again tonight & got cold.

June 1st, 1876. Awoke at Reveille and found the ground covered with <u>snow</u> and it continued snowing more or less all day and was cold & disagreeable. We occupied the cook tent nearly all day. I finished *Harper's* monthly for May, '76.

We did not move camp on account of the snow.

---

[6] Lieutenant Donald McIntosh (1838–June 25, 1876) was killed during Reno's retreat from the valley to the bluffs. He was a Civil War veteran of mixed Native American and white heritage.

[7] Lieutenant James Garland Sturgis (1854–June 25, 1876) was the son of General Samuel Sturgis, nominal commander of the 7th Cavalry. His body was not identified after the battle.

[8] The woman Godfrey calls Mamma was his stepmother, Jane Goble (1821–1877). He was raised by her, as his father, Dr. Charles Moore Godfrey, married her when his son was only three.

[9] Guy Charles Moore Godfrey (1870–1905), son of the diarist, was later a surgeon and captain in the Army medical corps. He died of a self-inflicted gunshot wound to the head while in service, leaving behind his wife and four-year-old son.

June 2nd. Still snowing a little & cold, passed time about as yesterday. Had water kegs filled with snow water.

June 3rd. Broke camp at 5 am and followed Stanley's '73 trail towards Beaver Creek. I am convinced that it would have been better to have kept on the foot of Sentinel Buttes. The roads were very good smooth rolling country. We had to make some crossings on account of the snow water. We got into camp about 4:30 on Beaver Creek. Plenty of wood & water. Scouts from Genl Gibbon[10] reported that he had not seen any body of Indians. Gibbon had had three stragglers killed.[11]

June 4th. We moved up Beaver Creek today and made a good march. Made camp at the same place Genl Stanley did in '72. Wood and water plenty. Our march has been very circuitous, unnecessarily so too I think. We saw pretty fresh buffaloe [*sic*] signs and some pretty fresh Indian signs too. Company is picket company today and will have to post them. There is absolutely a dearth of news or gossip. Genl Terry had Sun stroke today. Our road was good today and being on pioneer duty had only three crossings to make.

June 5th. We reached the Hd [head]waters of Beaver Creek today and at 8:30 came upon the Bad Lands on the headers of Cabin Creek. Beaver Creek is different from most of the streams and has no Bad lands on its headers The bad lands here however are not serious and we got along finely. We crossed one branch of Cabin Creek which had running water but very muddy and must be from the snows. We went two miles farther and went into camp near some pools. Good grazing & good water No wood No [?]. Today is Zoe's[12] birthday. Many a happy return!

---

[10] John Gibbon (1827–1896) was a career officer with a very distinguished Civil War record. On July 2, 1863, General George Gordon Meade had warned Gibbon at Gettysburg that if Lee were to attack the following day, it would be at the Union center—at Gibbon's forces. He was right. Gibbon was wounded that day and multiple times in the war. He shares with Custer the distinction of having been involved at Gettysburg and Little Bighorn. Gibbon also led troops in the Nez Perce war.

[11] This makes it sound like Gibbon ordered men in his command killed for straggling. Three men in Gibbon's column were ambushed and killed by Indians while hunting on May 23, 1876.

O'Fallon's Creek, M.T. *June 6th*. Two of Benteen's men who went out hunting yesterday a.m. and did not return last night; a beacon fire of sage brush was kept on a high hill hoping they might see it & be guided into camp. They joined us on the march today. An order was issued forbidding hunting parties to go out. We crossed two branches of O'Fallon's Creek, one a running stream. We have a very convenient camp for wood & water and plenty of grass. O'Fallon's Creek is a running stream with large pools of water. A little brackish.

June 7th. Powder River, M.T. We left camp at the usual hour and made a long detour down the creek and then followed up a branch of O'Fallon's Creek and then struck to the Divide of Powder River and followed that down several miles and then struck for the River. The Powder River hills are pretty high and are well wooded and afforded quite a relief to the monotony. We were unable to see the River or its line until within two miles of it. The road was very good for wagons with light loads but heavy loads would have consumed nearly two days and even more in bad weather.

June 8th. Powder River. We remained in camp today. Genl Terry with Keogh[13] & Moylan's[14] cos. went to the mouth of the River. We are making preparations for an 8 day's scout, all companies. Inf'y [to] escort the train. Had eleven pack mules & saddles turned over today had considerable amusement with the raw mules. One I had two water kegs put on—over and away he went bucking & jumping until he got one off and the other was thrown from one side to the other—another trial with two sacks of grain and they were torn and he got rid of that load and broke the saddle.[15]

---

[12] Zoe Godfrey Ogle (1855–1935), Godfrey's half-sister, married to Lt. Alexander Jackson Ogle.

[13] Myles Walter Keogh (1840–25 June 1876) was an Irish immigrant who served under Union cavalry commander John Buford during the Civil War. His service in that war was lauded highly by many in the Union high command. He rode the now-famous horse Comanche into battle at the Little Bighorn.

[14] Myles Moylan (1838–1909) was a career officer, Medal of Honor recipient (Bear Paw Mountain), and brother-in-law to James Calhoun of the 7th Cavalry.

[15] Terry later made the statement in his official report that his command was unused to employing pack mules. The mules they used were not

I had the aparejo & two boxes of ammunition [put on] and he succumbed without a struggle. We got a mail about 11 o'clock, one brought up by [the steamboat] *Far West*. Everybody well and Dooley improving—later in the day I got more mail and a letter from Genl Rice[16] informing me that he had gone to see Genl Sherman[17] and Sec. Taft[18] in my interest without my solicitation but not against my desires, however his mission was without success.

June 9th, 1876. Remained in camp today. Has been disagreeable & raining. Genl Terry came back late [or later?] and preparations have been made for a Scout but we don't know how many Cos or what ones go out. We are ordered to carry 2 days rations & forage on horses, 100 rounds of carbine ammunition on person, six days rations & forage on pack mules: forage rations to be two pounds and two boxes of ammunition on the pack mule.

June 10th. Today orders have been issued for six Cos B, C, E, F, I & L (right wing) under Col. Reno to go on a scout, provided with 12 days rations and forage. It has been a subject of conversation among officers why Genl Custer was not in command[19] but no solution yet has been arrived at. All Cos of the left wing have been ordered to turn over to the other six Cos all rations but one day & four (4) pack mules & saddles. We have been ordered to accompany the wagon train down to the mouth of Powder River. Saw Porter about the box

---

trained to carry but used to pull the wagons, thus were quite put out to be saddled with an aparejo (a packsaddle made of a stuffed leather pad) and loaded down with freight. See *The Terry Diary: Battle of the Little Bighorn* (2014, BIG BYTE BOOKS).

[16] Edmund Rice (1842–1906) was a career soldier and a Medal of Honor recipient. He served in the Civil War, Indian Wars, Spanish American War and Philippine War.

[17] William Tecumseh Sherman (1820–1891) was Commanding General of the Army under President Grant.

[18] Alphonso Taft (1810–1891) was Secretary of War in 1876 and soon to become Grant's Attorney General.

[19] Terry's diary of the expedition make it clear he was annoyed with Custer for not staying with the command and instead scouting out far ahead; Terry admonished Custer to stay with the command. It could be as well that he was concerned that Custer would find the Indians and take the initiative to attack.

of cake sent us by our wives & [he] will get it for us. The right wing got off about 3 p.m.

June 11th. Broke camp at 6 a.m. late on a/c of rain. We had to let the canvass dry out. The roads were pretty heavy and some pretty difficult hills to contend with; also my pack mules were of some trouble at first. But after three miles travel the train arrived on a level plateau and went swooping over so that, as I was rear guard, I got over three miles behind, waiting on the pack train. Got into camp at 7:30. 24 miles.

June 12. Remained at Powder River. Got a letter off [to] Mary and Guy.

June 13, 14 & 15. Camp at Powder River.

June 16. [*unreadable*] Left camp at 6 a.m. We had considerable trouble getting our packs ready but got them off in pretty good order. The first part of the day we had considerable trouble. They were all placed under charge of Lt. Hare[20] and kept to the rear. We did not know much about packing but my own Company got along better than most of them. The road (South side of Yellowstone) was very fair and I think by keeping about four or five miles from the river, where the bluffs first run into the River a wagon train could get along very well. We got into camp at 4:30 p.m. We lunched opposite Genl Stanley's Camp of '73 at 12 o'c. Marched about 28 miles.

June 17.[21] Raining this a.m. broke camp at 6 a.m. and reached Tongue River at 8:30 a.m., much sooner than I anticipated and went into camp and about 12 the boat came up.

June 18. The command remained in camp. I got permission from Genl Terry to go up on the boat to the mouth of Tongue River. I spent a very pleasant day; played whist with Gibbs[22] against Genl

---

[20] Luther Rector Hare (1851–1929) was a friend and second in command of Godfrey's company.
[21] Unbeknownst to Terry and his entire command, General Crook engaged the large force led by Crazy Horse on Rosebud Creek on this day and was forced to withdraw. If that intelligence had come to Terry, Gibbon, and Custer, the events of June 25 would likely have been different.

Terry and [Captain O.E.] Machailes. We were victorious, although I am sure they had the science on us.

June 19th. Remained in camp and played whist with Weir,[23] Machailes, and Edgerly.[24] Scouts came this p.m. and reported Col. Reno coming up the Yellowstone about 8 or 10 miles. Great excitement among the men.

The command moved up the Yellowstone to the Tongue.

June 20. Broke camp at about 8 a.m. Went up Tongue River a mile or two to cross and found a good ford. About 11:30 we reached Col. Reno's camp; soon after the boat came. Col. Reno's scout did not give any definite results. He went up the Powder River and over to Tongue and thence to Rose Bud. He did not see any Indians nor game but reports a ~~old~~ camp about three weeks old of about 350 lodges.[25] We broke camp at 4 p.m. I was Rearg'd [rear-guarded] and had anything but a pleasant time of it. We marched over the bluffs through some very <u>bad</u> lands and got into camp 11 p.m. had supper and retired. Distance (whole day), 25 miles.

June 21. Broke camp at 6 a.m. The Yellowstone looks very pretty with her wooded islands. We went into camp at 12:30. The 2nd Cav. marched up the opposite side of Yellowstone just as we went down the bluffs. Saw Genl Gibbon & Brisbin[26] on boat—a conference was

---

[22] William Gibbs (1845–1934) was a private under Godfrey's command.

[23] Captain Thomas Benton Weir (1838–December 9, 1876) was probably as much a casualty of the Battle of the Little Bighorn as the men who died on June 25th. Weir had served under Custer in the Civil War. On June 25th, 1876 he made an unauthorized advance along the bluffs to search for Custer's companies. He died in December of complications of alcoholism.

[24] Winfield Scott Edgerly (1846–1927) was a second lieutenant in Company D. A career soldier, he served in the Indian Wars (he was at Wounded Knee), the Spanish American War, in the Philippines, and retired a brigadier general.

[25] Custer was disgusted that Reno had gone as far as the Rosebud, not engaged the Indians, and that he might have given the Indians notice of their presence. He also thought Reno missed a chance at distinction by not pursuing the trail and striking the Indians. Terry was angry at Reno for exceeding his orders by going all the way west to the Rosebud.

[26] James Sanks Brisbin (1837–1892) was an educator, lawyer, historian, author, and soldier. He wrote a famous letter to Godfrey after the latter

held and it was decided that our Regt move at 12 tomorrow up the Rose Bud—the 2nd Cav. to X the Yellowstone at Fort Pease and move up the Big Horn & "Little" Horn. We had our Hard Bread assorted and everything preparatory to starting.

June 24. While the officers were separating at the "Sundance" camp Genl Custer's guidon fell down to the rear. I picked it up & stuck in the ground. Soon it fell again to the rear; this time I stuck it in some sage brush & ground so that it stuck. I never thought of it again till after the fight when my attention was called to it by Lt. Wallace[27] who seems to have regarded it as a bad omen.

The paragraph above was inserted on the page post-battle. Note the date. He drew a pencil line across the page below the June 21 entry and wrote this paragraph on the bottom quarter of the page. The "Sun Dance" camp was a Sioux camp at which the regiment stopped on its way up the Rosebud and where the Sioux had conducted a Sun Dance. It was there that Sitting Bull had his vision of soldiers falling upside down into the Indian camp. The next paragraph resumes the chronology as originally written.—Ed. 2014

June 22. We left the Yellowstone at 12 [noon] with 15 days rations of Hard Bread, Coffee & Sugar & 12 days bacon. Genls Terry, Gibbon,[28] & Custer reviewed the Regt as we left camp. The comd marched in column of fours. The Packs gave a great deal of trouble and some broke down just as we were leaving camp. We marched up the ~~right~~ left bank of the Rose Bud about 12 or 14 miles & went into camp about 4 p.m. After supper all officers reported at Hdqrs where we were informed that there would not be any more calls by trumpet, that Reveille would be at 3 & move at 5. That marches

---

published his 1892 *Century* article, telling Godfrey that Terry had been very anxious about Custer and the 7th from the time they left the Yellowstone to go up the Rosebud. Brisbin had offered troops from his 2nd Cavalry to Custer but the latter refused them.

[27] George Daniel Wallace (1849–1890) commanded Company G. He died from gunshot wounds at the Wounded Knee massacre.

[28] Gibbon later wrote, "Custer shook hands with us and bade us good-by. As he turned to leave us I made some pleasant remark, warning him against being greedy, and with a gay wave of his hand he called back, 'No, I will not.'" ("Last Summer's Expedition Against the Sioux," Gibbon, *American Catholic Quarterly Review*, 1877.

would be of easy stages from 25 to 30 miles a day. I went to bed soon after the officers were dismissed, after giving orders and looking at herd.

I walked back with Wallace who said he believed Genl Custer would be killed as he had never heard him talk as he did, or his manner so subdued.

June 23. We got off from camp with our packs on time & everything went very smoothly. After marching about 8 miles we came across a very large village grounds and during the day we passed two more camps, all indicating a very large number of Indians. The valley of the Rose Bud is quite well wooded and generally a thick undergrowth of Rose bushes. The creek is well named. 33 or 35 miles.

June 24. We passed a very large camp about 7:30 and officers call was sounded. The poles of the Lodge for the "Sun Dance" was [sic] standing They had evidently had a big time. Also was found a whiteman's [sic] scalp not quite dry. It was estimated as consisting of three or four hundred lodges. The Crow scouts were very active and were busy. Went on carefully until sundown when we went into a camp and at 11:30 p.m. took up our line of march again and continued until about 2 o'clock when we halted to await the arrival of news from Lt. Varnum[29] & Crow scouts who had been sent ahead.

June 25. After daylight we unsaddled and made coffee. About 8 a.m. scout came with news that they had discovered a village and could see smoke, although Varnum said he could not distinguish anything. We continued our march. Genl Custer came around personally and informed us that the Sioux village was in view. I did not see Genl & so when told by Burckhardt that he had been around & left that information, I mounted & went to Hdqrs to hear the news.

---

[29] Charles Albert Varnum (1849–1936) was the chief of scouts on the expedition. He had been up to the divide between the Rosebud and the Little Bighorn Valley early that morning and was informed by the scout that there was an enormous Indian village about 15 miles away. Varnum commanded a company of the 7th Cavalry at Wounded Knee and received a Medal of Honor for action at Drexel Mission.

Bloody Knife[30] was talking to the Genl & said we would find enough Sioux to keep us fighting two or three days; Genl remarked laughingly that he thought we would get through in one day. We took up our line of march to within a couple of miles of the Divide between "Rose Bud" & "Little Big Horn" when we halted and hid in a ravine. Soon after Col. Keogh came & reported that Sergt. Curtis[31] had seen an Indian getting hard bread from a box that had been lost during the night. The Indian ran away when he saw the Sergt and party. The Crow scouts had seen some Indians also and thought they had seen the dust of the command and were aware of our presence in the country. ~~Cook~~ Tom Custer went immediately to inform Genl what had been seen and Genl came to where we were in bivouac. The Genl had been with the Crow scouts on the watch [the Crow's Nest overlook] while we were in camp. Genl had officers call sounded. We were informed of what had happened and that the impression was that the village was about 15 miles off and that we would start immediately. Co commanders were authorized to leave six men & 1 N. C. O. with the packs and that Cos would move out in the order of reports of Co. Commdrs that their Cos were ready. I went to see if everything was ready & I reported just as McIntosh reported but Cook[32] recognized him first & so I came in No. 10.

I thought I certainly would be of the advance but some Co. Comdrs reported without seeing to anything and so got the lead. After we arrived at the summit of the Divide between Rose Bud & L.B. Horn I received an order to report to Col. Benteen for duty with his Battln. He was ordered to scout toward the L.B.H. and above the creek valley down which the main command of Genl Custer was marching. After wandering among the hills without any probability of accomplishing anything we went into the valley [Col. Benteen

---

[30] Bloody Knife (*NeesiRAhpát*; ca. 1840–June 25, 1876) was Custer's favorite of the Arikara scouts, reportedly because he didn't mince words with the general. He was shot in the head while Reno was in the timber in the Little Bighorn Valley after being driven there by the warriors. Being close to Reno, Bloody Knife's brains and blood spattered on the major.
[31] William A. Curtis (1846–1888) was sergeant of Company F.
[32] This was Custer's adjutant, William Winer Cooke (1846–June 25, 1876) who later that day wrote the famous "Benteen, come on" note. Godfrey consistently spells it "Cook."

received a note from Col. Cook that the village was in front & to bring up the packs. *brackets in original*]. I did not hear any firing and when we passed an old village I concluded from the age of the trail that we had a march of 18 to 20 miles before we would reach any village and that they would have seen us. This was about four miles from where the village was located Soon after we passed the old village camp, we watered our horses.[33] This was about 2 o'clock p.m. After we watered, we continued our march very leisurely. Not long after watering the trumpeter brought the note from Col. Cook above noted[34] (in brackets) and we increased our gait.

We heard occasional shots and I concluded the fight was over; that [we] had nothing to do but go up and congratulate the others & help destroy the plunder. The firing became more distinct, and we increased our gait—a Sergt[35] of one of the companies passed us & remarked "We've got them boys" I thought all was over & that it could only have been a small village to be over so soon.

We soon came in sight of the valley of Little Big Horn River and its wide bottom was covered with horsemen who I at first thought to be our own command.

I saw a company on the hills which I supposed to be there for picket duty while the others were destroying the village. Some Crow Indian scouts came up over the hills driving a herd of ponies and soon came to us and I asked by signs which way we could go down to the bottom or get to the command. He motioned to go to the right, and I told Col. Benteen so we went that way a short distance and soon came to where Col. Reno with his Cos A, G, and M were. Hare came up soon & said that Cos M, A, & G had charged over the plain, that they had a big fight in the woods above the village, and were whipped out, that they were obliged to cut their way through, and

---

[33] At what students and scholars of the fight call "the morass," which is how the witnesses at the Reno Court of Inquiry termed it. See *Reno Court of Inquiry* (2015, BIG BYTE BOOKS).

[34] This was the famous last message from Custer: *Benteen, come on. Big village. Be quick. Bring packs. P.S. bring paks.*

[35] Sergeant Daniel Kanipe (1853–1927) actually passed them before John Martin came with the note. Records show that although his name was spelled Kanipe, he served in the 7th Cavalry as Knipe.

were "d—d glad to see us." We formed a dismounted skirmish line along the crest of the bluffs where we afterwards intrenched ourselves. Singular to us it appeared that they [the Indians] made no demonstration against us. We were watching anxiously for our pack train with the reserve ammunition for the three Cos had expended nearly all they had on their persons in the woods below—in the meantime Col Reno sent one Co. to some bluffs lower down to look for Genl Custer.[36] We heard volley firing and the rattle of the guns. They returned soon after without any tidings of Genl Custer—we thought it very strange that he [Custer] did not make his way back to us. So, soon after the packs got up, we mounted and moved towards where Genl Custer was supposed to be. We got on some very high bluffs and large numbers of Indians were seen on some bluffs about two miles away but the firing had ceased except an occasional shot. Upon our appearance at the bluffs the Indians directed their attention towards us, and large numbers almost immediately ran toward us. On their approach it was evident they meant business and Col Benteen suggested that we get back to the place where we first threw out skirmishers so as to throw ourselves into position to receive them and protect our stock. The packs were moved and all Cos except Weir, French,[37] & mine. Weir, & French were on a very high ridge, I was along the crest of the bluffs toward the river. I was dismounted. As soon as Weir & French began their retreat the Indians followed to the high point and I received orders to mount and move in to the camp. I had not gone far when I saw the Indians would make sad havoc in the other Cos unless checked, so I dismounted & formed skirmish line for their protection while they retreated into the lines, and sent my led horses in. The fire of the Indians was very hot, and they sent many a bullet about us but fortunately none of us were hit. Of D and M two or three wounded & one killed[38] who fell in the hands of the enemy. A number of horses

---

36 Reno did not send them; Captain Weir made an unauthorized movement down to what is now Weir Point. Godfrey got his timing wrong above in that nearly all the companies followed in Weir's path before hastening back to the swale where they spent the next two days.

37 Thomas Henry French (1843–1882) was a Civil War veteran and captain of M Company.

38 Farrier, Vincent Charley (b. Vinzenz Schärli; 1849–June 25, 1876) was

were wounded. I got an order to fall back to the lines and in so doing the line of skirmishers began to go a little faster & faster and to get into groups I halted them & cautioned that the Indians had a better chance to hit them. Another attempt & the same result soon followed when I halted them then again, as I was determined to not let them have any panic. Many had not been under fire before. We retreated again & got into the lines & laid down. Soon the Indians followed to the ridge. My presence outside had protected, and we gave them a reception with such warmth that they did not attempt again to come nearer than the ridge in numbers or mounted. We all knew then is [sic] meant a siege for a time at least and so the best was done for our horses & packs. They were put in a ravine[39] and a skirmish line formed on three sides of it and the Indians seeing the openness of the fourth side got to where they could shoot directly into the herd. The packs were then unloaded and used for a breastwork, and Moylans Co was inside of it. Benteen was on the crest of the bluffs on the upper side of the ~~river~~ camp[?]. "B" co was on his right lower down and the line continued from left to right. "M", G, D, and my Co was interpolated with the last three when I came in from the Skr [skirmish] line. Everybody now was required to be on their bellies or to lie close to the ground and the bullets came thick & fast. I felt that I ought to reassure the men, however, and so I kept moving about the lines, Hare & Edgerly asked me several times to lie down. I was standing over Sergt Winney,[40] talking to somebody & giving orders when a bullet went through him. He gave a quick convulsive jerk, said "I am hit" and looked at me imploringly. I told him to lie down & be quiet until the fusillade was over when I would have him taken to the hospital[41] & he turned as if to do so, threw his weight on his elbows and was dead. This was

---

possibly identified by archaeologists (*Uncovering History*, Scott and Reece, 2013).

[39] Visitors to the battlefield today may be amazed to see the Reno-Benteen Defense Area is merely a shallow swale, not a ravine. The horses and mules were corralled in the center and were an open target to the Indians.

[40] Dewitt Winney (1845–1876) was first sergeant of K Company. Godfrey mentions later in the diary that he corresponded with Winney's brother.

[41] The "hospital" was just an area cleared within the herd where young Dr. Henry Porter was the sole physician left alive to treat the wounded.

the first time since 1861 that I had seen a man killed in battle yet I felt cool & unconcerned as to myself. Burckhardt,[42] my cook, was directly in rear of Sergt Winney, begged me to "Please lie down, Lieut.; you will get hit, Please, sir, lie down" & I did so; I found the Sergt was dead. I went back to a place immediately[?] in rear of the line. I was obliged [to] give my attention to the use of ammunition; if allowed, the men would fire all the time at random. I also found my movements were attracting the attention of the Indians and that I was endangering others. As soon as I laid down I said my prayers & went to sleep.[43]

A vigorous fire by the Indians wakened me; we made a sally [charge] and every man but one of D co. moved out of the line. We drove the [sic] back the Indians and took our ~~ridge~~ position again. The "D" Co man was killed directly after the troops laid down. How I did wish Genl Custer would return. It looked very much like a siege and as a matter of course our thoughts turned to the future. It was my opinion we ought to fold up our tents and silently steal away. Col Weir came to where I was and we talked the matter over. My reasons for moving were that I thought Genl Custer was below us and we could join him; that we had no water & a few wounded; that we would have our casualties & burdens increased on the morrow; that I did not think the Indians would force an engagement during the night. We both thought that to Col Benteen we must look for the wisdom to deliver us from our situation or defend us as it was evident that Col Reno carried no vigor nor decision, and his personal behavior gave no confidence in him.

The firing ceased from the Indians at dark, and I made the men go to work digging out pits. The ground was very hard clay and it was with great difficulty we got them finished.

I had my packs & bedding brought from the "corral" or herd and made into a barricade where Mr. Hare & myself laid down & slept. We opened a can of California Pears and they were very refreshing.

---

[42] Charles Burkhardt (1846–1888)

[43] This may seem odd but there are many reports of soldiers during the Civil War even falling asleep next to firing artillery due to exhaustion. By the 25th, the command had had little rest since leaving the Yellowstone.

A few shots were fired during the night and scouts were ordered out to open communication with Genl Custer but returned saying the country was covered with Sioux. A visit to the Hospital made in the evening was very sad. There were quite a number of horses & mules killed. The Indians got the range of the herd from a ridge about four hundred yards off and did considerable execution.[44]

It was at my suggestion that "D" Co was moved down to cover the line opposite the River.[45] Our troops did not do as much firing as ought to have been done so that their range was pretty accurate and their aim not at all disturbed. I thought we were a little too niggardly of our ammunition and determined tomorrow to have good shots[46] do some work. I wished very much for Pvt Clear[47] who was one of the best shots & was killed while with Mr. Hare, with Col Reno [in the valley]. We have not had any water since we got into position and am quite dry. I have kept my cigar out of my mouth and kept the men from using tobacco as much as possible.

Monday, June 26, 1876. The firing began at an early hour, before it was fairly daylight, by the Indians and according to determination by my men to let them know we were on hand, I permitted different men of the Co. to fire at times. I watched with interest & amusement how some would aim. I generally told them what range to fire at and afterwards only allowed the best shots to fire. Pvts. Madden[48] & Lasley[49] were about the coolest and best shots. About 11 I sent a detail with canteens to get water. They were not successful but learning that Col Benteen would send a detail down under cover of his fire, another detail was made. I did not eat anything this morning until about 9 o'clock when I got very hungry & felt

---

[44] Now known as Sharpshooter's Ridge.
[45] The eastern, most open side of the swale.
[46] By "good shots" he means marksmen.
[47] Elihue Franklin Clear (1843–June 25, 1876) had been with the 7th Cavalry for nine years.
[48] Irish immigrant, Michael Madden (1848–1883) was severely wounded in the leg during the foray to get water from the river. Dr. Porter was obliged to perform a field amputation on Madden.
[49] William Walker Lasley (1842–1924) had served in a Confederate infantry regiment (10th Missouri) and served later served in the Spanish American War and in the Philippines.

exhausted. I happened to think of some raw potatoes I had in a sack & tried one with some hard bread. I found it quite a relief and gave some out. I got a sip of water from Wallace who had his canteen filled. My detail came back after an hour's absence with some canteens & said the rest had been taken at the hospital; also that Pvt. Madden was wounded with his leg broken. I sent a detail to get him up from the River near which he was placed but they were not permitted to go down. The Indians kept up a very heavy fire on all who went after water. After about 3 p.m. there was very little firing, except at this place but all had to hold the trenches. Pvts Corcoran[50] & Mielke[51] were wounded during the day. Pretty early in the morning they [the Indians] made quite a determined advance on both sides of camp and kept a pretty vigorous fire from the hills too. We met them on one side by a heavy fire and they retired. On Col Benteen's line they kept advancing until they got almost to the top of the hill when Col Benteen charged his men on them & drove the Indians back. Soon after Col Benteen came over & asked for more men. I expected my Co to be sent over but French was sent over. Both Co's had a good many wounded men. Col Benteen ordered us to charge although Col Reno was then on the line. Col Reno went out with us and ordered us back to the trenches before we had gone twenty yards as the firing became very warm & there was no breast work to hide behind. But still it had its effect and we kept up a pretty warm fire too. About 7 p.m. we saw the Indian village moving. It was or seemed to be about 3 miles long by ¾ wide and very closely packed. It was about 1-1/2 miles from where we were. They did not seem to be in any haste and moved off orderly, a few remained in the bottom out of our range until nearly dark. We surmised that their ammunition was giving out and they intended to move their village to a safe distance and on 27th to make a more vigorous assault[52] or else that Genl Custer was coming to our assistance with reinforcements. We moved our lines at dark to a more advantageous

---

[50] Patrick Corcoran (1844–1922) was from Canada. He applied for an invalid pension in 1877.
[51] Max Mielke (1845–1877) was a German immigrant, only in the regiment since March. He was killed the next year at Bear Paw Mountain.
[52] In fact, the Indians had scouts out and knew that Generals Terry and Gibbon were coming up the Little Bighorn Valley.

point & where our stock would be under better protection and where we could get water. We endeavored to get our stock down to the river that night but no place was found where it was practicable. I got a cup of coffee with French & after seeing the men at their work in the pits I went to bed with Wallace & Hare in my pit. I had not had my clothes off for three days & I felt tired, worn, dirty & sleepy.

June 27, 1876. I was awakened by the reveille and felt better to know that at daylight the Indians did not fire the morning guns. I had coffee & breakfast prepared, the stock attended to. No settled purpose seems to have been made, we feel that something has disturbed the Indians but the direction does not show [*unreadable*] Gen Crook. About 9 a.m. whilst discussing the probabilities it was the general opinion that the Indians had some kind of a trap or had run out of ammunition. It was intended to send out couriers to communicate with Genl Terry who was supposed to be coming up to the mouth of the Little Horn. These couriers had been sent out last night but came back saying that the Sioux were still about the camp and [the couriers] would not go out. No Indians have been seen. A few ponies are to be seen grazing below in the bottom. About 9:30 a.m. cloud of dust was seen several miles below camp, and everybody was called to his place. The horses were taken into the ravine between the lines and I sent camp kettles, canteens, &c., to the river to have them filled; preparations were made that we might be prepared in case it should prove they were Indians. An hour of suspense was passed when it was finally settled they were our own troops. Then speculation was rife as to whose column it was. We looked in vain for a company of white horses[53] so we gave up that it was Genl Custer and thought then it might be Genl Crook, but a <u>hearty cheer</u> went up from the throats of our gallant men, for we knew we were delivered from our foes. Soon a scout came up with a note from Genl Terry to Genl Custer saying some [of] our Crow scouts gave the information that we were whipped and nearly all killed, that he did not believe the story but he was bringing medical assistance. This note was written on 26th and the scout said he could not get in to our camp the night before as the Sioux were on

---

53 E-Company's greys had been with Custer.

the alert. At reveille Lt. De Rudio[54] came into camp. He had been in the woods in river bottom for two days. His horse got away from him as the Cos were coming out of the fight under Col Reno and he was obliged to take refuge in the woods. With him were F. Girrard,[55] interpreter,—Jackson,[56] a half breed scout & Pvt. O'Neal [sic], Co. G. During the first night Girrard & Jackson, who were mounted, got separated from the others but all got in O.K.

Lt. Bradley[57] 7th Infty came up next & made inquiry as to how I was from some of our fellows & soon I met him. The first thing I asked was where Genl Custer was and he told me he did not know but supposed him killed, as he had counted 197 bodies he did not think any of them had escaped. I was dumbfounded—for indeed there did not seem to be any hope except that some of them had cut their way through to the prairie and gone down the River. The three Crow scouts had given correct information as to Genl Custer's column. It did seem so impossible. Genl Terry & staff soon came upon the scene & was greeted with hearty cheers by all. Scarcely a word was spoken by the officers, but a handshake gave token of our thankfulness for relief, and our silence spoke deeper than words our grief for the dead. The oppressiveness of our situation was fully realized and tears filled nearly every eye. The rest of the day was spent in making preparations to take the wounded down below

[54] Charles Camillo DeRudio (b. Carlo Camillo Di Rudio; 1832–1910) was an Italian aristocrat, would-be assassin of Napoleon III, and a career Army officer. He was known by some in the command as "Count No-Account" due to his wild stories. DeRudio and Pvt. Thomas O'Neill had spent 36 hours trying to find the command.
[55] Fredric Frances Gerard (1829–1913) was a frontiersman, army scout, and civilian interpreter. He testified at the 1879 Reno Court of Inquiry, where Reno's defense counsel attempted to disparage Gerard by raising the issue that he'd been married to an Indian woman.
[56] William "Billy" Jackson (*Sik-si-ka'-kwan* or Blackfoot Man) was a well-known scout and interpreter at the time.
[57] Chief of scouts for Gibbon, James Bradley (1844–1877), also kept a diary of the during the expedition. Bradley and his scouts were the first to come upon the dead on the Custer battlefield. He was a fine writer and historian, and was preparing his diary for publication the next year when he was killed at the Battle of Big Hole. Bradley was only 17 when he volunteered in the Civil War and he served the entire war. See *The Montana Column: March to the Little Bighorn* (2015, BIG BYTE BOOKS).

where the comnd was encamped. I went down & met a number of officers of cav & Infty while down with the wounded. Sergt Madden has his leg cut off.[58]

June 28th. We broke camp and went to the scene of Genl Custers disaster for the purpose of burying the dead. We found the bodies strewn from a few hundred yards of the ford up to a ridge. We buried as nearly as I can count 212 bodies including Genl Custer, whose face & expression was natural. Tom Custer, Cook, & Riley[59] were all the officers I recognized. Others recognized Yates,[60] Keogh, Calhoun[61], Crittenden[62] & Smith.[63] The bodies of Porter,[64] Jack Sturgis, Harrington[65] & Dr. Lord[66] were not recognized. While the bodies were being buried I went to right about 1-1/2 miles to see if I could discover any more bodies. I thought I traced the tracks of our horses but everything indicated a pursuit—that is, a rapid march. I found a gray horse[67] with an Indian bridle, halter & lariat. The horse

---

[58] Twenty-eight year old assistant surgeon, Henry Rinaldo Porter (1848–1903), was the only surviving physician on June 25th. He did an extraordinary job of tending to over fifty wounded all the way back to Fort Lincoln. He later established a thriving practice in Bismarck, Dakota Territory. He died and is buried in Agra, India, where he was visiting on a round-the-world trip in 1903.

[59] William Van Wyck Reily (1853–June 25, 1876) was 2nd lieutenant of Company F.

[60] George Walter Yates (1843–June 25, 1876) was the captain of Company F.

[61] James Calhoun (1845–June 25, 1876) was 1st lieutenant of Company C and was married to Custer's sister Margaret.

[62] John Jordan Crittenden III (1854–June 25, 1876) had only joined the 7th Cavalry six days before its departure from Ft. Lincoln. He was identified by broken pieces of his glass eye.

[63] Algernon Emory Smith (1842–June 25, 1876) commanded the Gray Horse Troop or Company E. He was a veteran of the Civil War.

[64] James Ezekiel Porter (1847–June 25, 1876) was 1st lieutenant of Company I.

[65] Henry Moore Harrington (1849–June 25, 1876) was 2nd lieutenant of Company C.

[66] George Edwin Lord (1846–June 25, 1876) was the Army assistant surgeon assigned to Custer's column on the day of the battle.

[67] There is some question today whether this gray was, like Comanche, a survivor of the battle. There is a picture some years later of Comanche with a gray horse with no explanation as to why that horse is in the picture.

had a tuft of grass tied in his mouth to keep him from neighing. I took him in. We marched through the village and camped below the other troops.

June 29. We remained in camp.

June 30. Crossed the L.B.H. in afternoon & camped & mustered. In the evening we took up our march for the mouth of Little Big Horn and got to the boat at 2:30 am. Sent a dispatch via Ellis.[68]

July 1st. Left L.B.H. & marched down Big Horn 20 miles. Route very rough—impracticable for wagons.

July 2nd. Continued our march down; followed the divide between B.H. and Tullock's creek. Very good cav. road but impracticable for wagons. A wagon train would be obliged to go up on left side of B.H. or follow Tullocks—26 miles & crossed on steamboat to old Battle ground of Big Horn of '73.

Wrote [*inserted:* to *illegible*] mail to leave on boat for Lincoln with dispatches. We got quite

July 3rd. We got quite a mail today of papers. The letters we got yesterday, all well. The boat left at noon. Col Smith went with dispatches & Baker with his Co as escort—I gave him my letters to Darlings. We found one of the Crow scouts [Curley] who was with Genl Custer's command who says all our men fought to the death and describes Cook horse & says he was the bravest man he ever saw. He says no man escaped but himself, that a number were killed some distance from the main command. Called on 2nd Cav. Lts. Schofield[69] & McClernand[70] called this evening. It turns out that nearly all the Ree[71] scouts have returned to Powder River & safe.[72]

---

[68] In the original diary, this section was written above July 29 but Godfrey apparently later felt the chronology was incorrect. He drew lines around this section with an arrow, indicating it belonged under July 30.
[69] Richmond McAllister Schofield (1867–1941) was the son of John McAllister Schofield, Civil War general, Secretary of War under Johnson, and Commanding General of the Army.
[70] Edward John McClernand (1848–1936) received the Medal of Honor for actions the next year at Bear Paw Mountain. He was the son of politician and Civil War general John Alexander McClernand. Edward served in the Spanish American War and in the Philippines, retiring a brigadier general.

July 4th. All quiet today; no news,—no excitement. I wrote out an application on 3rd for a transfer to L Co & handed it to Col Reno who declined to approve for the reason that somebody would be promoted, but finally said he would transfer me if anybody was transferred who was not in the fight. I shall expect the Co., as Braden[73] will hardly be retired although he has been ordered before the retiring board—I withdrew my application.

July 5. Nothing new during day. In evening we were invited to Genl Terrys for a sing. After a pleasant social evening we visit 2nd Cav where the society was more convivial & kept it up till 12 midnight when we went to bed.

July 6. Some Crow Indians came in from Crow camp at Pryors Fork[74] & said Genl Crook had had a fight with Indians[75] on Tongue River on 17 & got turned back,—lost 19 m & 2 officers—the Crows all left them.

July 7th. A courier was dispatched to Genl Crook on 6th. Horse came in today.

July 8th. The courier returned having lost everything swimming Big Horn. He saw about 40 Indians—

July 9th. Got a letter from Mamma who says all well. The Indians attacked Lincoln & drove cattle away from Rice.[76] The letter was written on 24 & the fight took place on 25. Am officer of the Day. Lt. Bradley left this a.m. for Ellis.

Monday, July 10th. Visited pickets. Ball's[77] co. of 2nd came in from a scout to Pompeys Pillar.[78] He did not see any Indian signs

---

[71] Arikara scouts.

[72] Godfrey wrote across the top of two pages here: "Hayes of Ohio and Wheeler of NY nominees." The Republican convention was held June 14–16, 1876 and the nominees were Rutherford B. Hayes and William A. Wheeler.

[73] Charles Braden (1847–1919) was 1st Lieutenant of Company L. He had been severely wounded in the thigh while on the Yellowstone Expedition of 1873 with Custer, a wound that would create a disability for life.

[74] Pryor Creek is about 50 miles west of the LBH battlefield.

[75] The Battle of the Rosebud. See Vaughn, *With Crook at the Rosebud.*

[76] Fort Rice (1864–1878).

but the Crows are moving down nearer to us. Saw the account of Crooks fight on 17th of June in N.Y. *Herald* of 24; from it appears he was somewhat worsted. We all consider that we were very lucky in not being gobbled up whilst intrenched.

Tuesday. July 11. We recd orders to have 100 rounds of ammunition issued to each man and carry 100 rds [rounds] on the mules. I find I can carry only six days rations on mules & no forage. Have been writing a letter to Mamma in anticipation of a mail.

Tuesday [sic; Wednesday] July 12. nothing transpired during the day till 6:30 pm an orderly brought an order to move at 7 am tomorrow. As soon as the orderly had delivered the message the "General" sounded and we packed & moved $1/_2$ mile down the river for better grass. After we got here everybody was in an ill humor about the camp. The bottom is broken up into a dust-heap—We've not had any rain for several weeks & the ground is very dry.

Wednesday, July 12th, 1876. [note date is same as previous entry] Read Mrs. Victor's[79] sketches of Oregon & Washington. Got information that a mail would leave for Ellis, but I don't think I'll send that way. 8 p.m., just learned that a mail would go down the river to Powder River in two hours. I hurriedly finished my letters to Mamma & Father also wrote Corpl Nolan to send my trunk & some stationary by boat & report how many boxes of ammunition were shipped by boat. I cannot find any at all in the pile of ordnance. After I got my letters sealed, I went over to put in the mail. Capt Ball, Lts. Hamilton & Roe[80] & Dr. Paulding[81] were at Hdqtrs & several of our officers congregated & we had a very pleasant time singing until 11:30 perhaps a little later.

---

[77] Captain Edward Ball.

[78] See https://www.blm.gov/visit/pompeys-pillar-national-monument.

[79] Frances Auretta Fuller Victor (1826–1902) was an American historian and novelist.

[80] Charles Francis Roe (1848–1922). In July 1881, Roe led a troop of soldiers to erect the monument that still stands on Last Stand Hill at the Little Bighorn National Monument.

[81] Captain Holmes Offley Paulding (1853–1883) was the surgeon with Gibbon's command.

July 13 Thursday Read in "Oregon" &c and then went a fishing; after an hour fish, went in the river bathing. The water is still very cold; caught one <u>little</u> fish. Soon after lunch a thunder storm gave us about 1/2 to 2/3 in. of rain—which refreshes the atmosphere and laid the dust. Took a ride to the boat & after retreat walked down again. Nothing new.

Friday July 14. Great clouds of grasshoppers have made their appearance and seem to be traveling down the river. A number of Crow Indians are looked for tomorrow.[82] Took a walk down to the boat and walked about to see her defences. The Pilot House is surrounded with 1' 5 in. oak, and there are cottonwood logs laid parallel & against the steam pipes. Cottonwood logs are placed vertically about the engineers stand. The cabin is really the most dangerous part to remain in, in case of an attack by Indians, as the thin pine boards would give little or no protection except to <u>hide</u>. A most terrific thunderstorm after dark.

Saturday July 15th. The Crow scouts were about the camp early. Visited Col. Benteen & Capt. Sanno,[83] 7th Infty. Saw Sergt. Becker's[84] map of the Battle field. That part of the map showing Genl Custer's force may be correct but that representing the siege ground is not correct. He showed me where there had been camped, or supposed, the Arapahoes. It was on three sides of a square the fourth side being filled in by the lodges of the chiefs.[85] It was cut out of the woods and seems was not seen by anyone else and in it were the bodies of three (3) whites.

Capt. Machailes' Ord. off. came up to camp with dispatch from Genl Sheridan dated July 8, Phila. recd at Bozeman M.T., July 12.

---

[82] These were scouts for the Army.

[83] James M. J. Sanno (1840–1907) was a career officer and veteran of the Civil War, Indian Wars, Spanish American War, and the Philippine War. General Gibbon recommended that Sanno receive the Medal of Honor for actions at the Battle of Big Hole in 1877.

[84] This is the Maguire Map. Godfrey's statement that it didn't correctly depict features correctly was later echoed by witnesses at the Reno Court of Inquiry. The map was very hastily drawn prior to the forces leaving the scene after the battle. It can easily be found online.

[85] Godfrey drew a tiny facsimile here of what he described.

The couriers brought the mail down too & came in a boat, yawl or skiff. 6 cos. of (5th Infty)?[86] are ordered from Dept of Mo. & he has applied for 6 Cos of 22nd.

Went down to the boat. There I found them unloading and that it would start down the river tomorrow for Bismarck.[87] All this in consequence of Genl Sheridan's dispatch.

Sunday, July 16th, 1876. Got up & had breakfast at 7 am. Wrote to Mamma & Mage Rice. Gave Mage a short a/c of the battle and twitted him on our enormous army & expressed the hope that if the army should be reduced "Lineal promotion" be made one of the provisions and congratulated him on his renomination & hoped for his reelection which is pretty sure. Wrote to Mamma that I thought we would be out a long time & she had better go home & see the folks. I enclosed a check for $253.85 on 1st National Yankton, D.T. Asked Col Reno if he objected to my going down to Lincoln "Yes! if we find where Crook is we'll go to him.", it would have given me great joy to have gone down & seen my darlings.

The boat got off about 11:30 a.m. Genl Terry, Col. Benteen went down to meet *Far West* & Sanger[88] & Moylan to Powder River to bring up wagon train. Went to Genl Gibbons tent & read *Army and Navy Journal* & debate on army appropriation. The action is disheartening. A number of officers 2nd Cav. came down & we had a jolly sing.

Monday, July 17. This is the anniversary of my first fight, at "Scareytown, W. Va." 1861.[89] Wrote to Hale today—a mail came in with a letter of 4th inst from darling Mamma & one of 25 ult. from Sister Eva.[90] They had not heard of battle of 25 & 26.

All [in the regiment] well & confident that if we struck the Indians we would beat them worse than Gen Crook did. "*L'homme propose et Dieu dispose.*"[91] He willed otherwise than they thought.

---

[86] Question mark in original.
[87] Which is across the river from Fort Lincoln.
[88] Louis H. Sanger (–1884) was captain of Company G, 17th Infantry.
[89] Godfrey served a short stint in the 21st Ohio Infantry during the Civil War and the Battle of Scary Creek was the regiment's first engagement.
[90] Evaline Godfrey Loy (1850-1893) was a half-sister.

Visited Hd. Qtrs, saw Dr. Williams, Thompson, Genl Gibbon &c. A despatch from E. W. Smith[92] for Genl Terry was opened by Genl Gibbon which says the distress at Lincoln [by the widows and orphans of the Little Bighorn disaster] was indescribable and heartrending. That the country was ablaze with indignation that such a disaster should occur, & that the campaign would be carried on, &c.

Tuesday, July 18. Reported as officer of the day—a mail came in from Ellis with Montana papers of 13th and 14th from which there appears to be great excitement & indignation on a/c of our defeat & the country alive to the necessities of our little army. It seems that the <u>Senate</u> will pass the appropriation bills as passed by the House. The conference now may agree to strike out the army reduction.

Wednesday July 19/76. Went with horses over on Island at 7 a.m. I found the herds [herders?] had gone & made them return & report in compliance with orders. This was done as a lesson, but was disapproved by Col Reno. Came home for lunch at 1 p.m. & heard that Capt. Thompson,[93] 2nd Cav. had committed suicide at 5:30 am. He was buried at 6:30 pm. He had been suffering from disease, consumption, the germs of which were laid in "Libby" Prison, Va. during the war. He had been sick two days.

I got some papers from Genl Gibbon Cinti *Com.*[94] Walked home with Edgerly who wants me to write to Mrs. G. to send word to Mrs. E. when she goes East & to stop with her.

---

[91] "Man proposes and God disposes."
[92] Edward Worthington Smith (1832–1883) was a Civil War veteran and was assistant adjutant general to General Terry in 1876. He later commanded the 22nd Infantry and was brevetted a brigadier general.
[93] Lewis Tappan Thompson (1838–1876) was a Civil War veteran. Pvt William Taylor (7th Cav.) later wrote, "No reason was known for this rash act, unless as it was believed by many and so stated in camp at the time, that the hardships of the campaign and the horrors of the Custer battlefield had, as it undoubtedly had done to others, unsettled his mind. It was not an uncommon thing to happen on that summer's campaign." *With Custer on the Little Bighorn*, 1996, Penguin.
[94] Cincinnati *Commercial*.

Thursday—July 20. About 1 am was awakened by shots; had company fall in & marched out to where stable guard was & learned that two or more Indians had passed near there. They were going slow but when challenged, laid whip & skipped out. I had the horses brought in. This morning McConnell[95] brought my lariat; it was cut in two places with a knife. He said the horses were loose when he went out & Dandy[96] was coming to the picket line followed by the pony. They were both hobbled or they would have been taken away. The Indians continued on down the line & passed by the lower picket. Pretty severe headache but walked to 2nd Cav.; and returned papers to Genl Gibbon. Indians saw tracks of about 30 hostiles.

Friday July 21, 1876. Awakened with a severe headache. Ate a light breakfast and loafed at Tom McDougall's[97] tent. Headache continued until evening, when I felt better, but my head was sore & in the evening went over to Col Reno's & read Genl Gibbons letter in which he takes a good deal of credit to himself for getting up to our command. Genl Brisbin was there too. He is a great talker.

Saturday. July 22. Ordered to move today to change camp to about 1 mile below Fort Pease.[98] Moved at 3:30 p.m. about 3 miles <u>towards home</u> to a much safer & comfortable camp. The bluffs are about 1 mile off. Soon after getting into camp the Crows saw several Indians on the bluffs & mounted, gave chase but soon came back, the Sioux having "vamosed."

Went up to Regtl Hdqrs where we had a <u>sing</u> & pleasant social time till 11:30. Lots of mosquitoes.

Sunday, July 23. This the Holy Sabath Day, but all work goes on the same, no variation; had a bower built over my tent & find it adds greatly to comfort; Capt. Wheelan,[99] Lts. Hamilton,[100] Doane & Low[101]

---

95 Wilson McConnell (1839–1906) was a private in Godfrey's company. He was in the hilltop fight at LBH.
96 One of General Custer's two campaign horses; the one he rode to his death was Vic.
97 Thomas Mower McDougal (1845–1909) was Captain of B Company. He was in charge of the packtrain on the day of the battle.
98 Fort Pease was just below the mouth of the Big Horn River on the Yellowstone.
99 James Nicholas Wheelan (1838–1922) was a captain in the 2nd Cavalry, a

with 2 cos 2nd Cav., a battery of Artillery & 25 Crows went out on a scout to meet Moylan.

Monday, July 24. Began a letter to Guy. It rained from about 4:30 pm till after dark. A scout came in from Genl Terry who is on the *Far West.* He says he had no news from Crook. The boat ought to be here tomorrow. Col. Reno was placed in arrest by Genl Gibbon. Capt. Sanno 7th Infty is in arrest also.

Tuesday, July 25. One of the pickets was drowned this a.m. whilst going out to his post; a ravine had about 3 feet of water when he came to his Breakfast, but when he went back there was nearly 10 feet of water & swift—he could not swim & it seems he was thrown from his horse. Col Reno got a copy of charges against him. It all comes from Col R sending out some scouts as videttes Saturday eve after we got into camp. I presume however Col Reno's manner has as much to do with the results, as his manner is rather aggressive & he protested against the scouts being taken from the Reg't.

The scouts came back from Gen. Crook [three (3) soldiers Co E 7th Inf & 4 Crows—*brackets in original*] who had left him on 23d. Genl Crook was 15 miles from Fort Kearney[102] waiting for the 5th Cav. to join him—he has supplies to Sept 30th; has been reinforced by 5 cos Infty. Genl Carr[103] 5th Cav captured 2 or 3 wagons of ammunition (escorted by 150 Indians) en route from Agcy to Hostiles. Wheelan came back having met the boat. The boat will be in tomorrow— Called on Sanno & several 7th foot gentlemen and then went down to Genl Gibbons tent. Genl Crook has not had a fight except having his pickets engaged & by scouting parties. One of his cos went out 23

Civil War veteran, and an overseas military attaché. He was eventually brevetted a brigadier general.

[100] Samuel T. Hamilton was 1st lieutenant of Company L, 2nd Cavalry.

[101] William Low, commander of the artillery detachment that included gatling guns, was said to have almost wept when he learned he had been excluded from the strike force that went up the Rosebud to the LBH (*A Terrible Glory*, Donovan, 2008).

[102] Crook has spent about five weeks on Goose Creek (location today in downtown Sheridan, Wyoming) mostly hunting and fishing.

[103] Eugene Asa Carr (1830–1910) was a career officer and Civil War veteran.

miles, became engaged on foot with one party, another party however got in their rear & stampeded their horses & they had to foot it back. They were of the 3rd Cav.[104]

Wednesday—July 25. Genl Terry arrived on boat *Far West.* I went down & was handed a letter by Mr. Burleigh, Clerk of boat. Col. Benteen also had my paper mail. 2 boxes of cigars (one for Hare) sent by my "darling." Genl Terry told me of their trip & time it took to cross over the train over three days, part of the time with two boats. I read part of Mamma's letter & put it up. I could not compose myself enough to read it on the boat so waited till I got to my tent. All was excitement about the Press news and opinions. I was reported to the Chicago *Times* as of the dead, probably through [*illegible*] Old Joe Tilford,[105] who seems to have been the informant & the <u>news</u> [may] have come from St. Louis

Thursday—July 27th. We broke camp at 10:30 & marched down the river about 5 miles. Crossed two bad ravines which had to be bridged. Dept. Hdqrs & Staff went down on the boat. We camped at the foot of the Ft. Pease bottom. Excellent grass. I marched on Off. [of the] Day yesterday & had two alarms today by the crows who were out hunting. Low, Doane and Roe visited me during the evening & we talked about West Point.

Friday July 28. Reveille at daylight. Infty & 2nd Cav. moved at 5:30, we at 7:30. The train had to take to the table land & experienced some difficulty getting up the hill. Our progress was very slow on a/c of the "Diamond R" teams[106] which moved like a

---

[104] This was the famous Sibley Scout. The horses were abandoned, not stampeded, in order to escape through the mountains. Two excellent first-person accounts can be read in Finerty, *On the Trail of Crazy Horse* (2017, BIG BYTE BOOKS) and *Legend: Life and Adventures of Frank Grouard* (2016, BIG BYTE BOOKS).

[105] Joseph Green Tilford (1829–1911) was a major with the 7th Cavalry but on leave during this campaign. He was later colonel (promoted brigadier general in 1891) of the 9th Cavalry Buffalo Soldier regiment.

[106] The Diamond R Freighting Company was contracted to haul supplies for Gibbon's Montana Column. See *Wagon Master: 1876 Sioux War Diary* (2016, BIG BYTE BOOKS). Matthew Carroll (1837–1909) was a principal of that company and kept a diary while freight master for Gibbon. Here Godfrey drew a small diamond enclosing an "R" within parentheses.

water wagon train. The teams are eight mules & two wagons coupled together. I think it requires an exceptionally good driver but fewer drivers are required. The weight is distributed over more surface, but again the weight is well behind the mules. We got to the Little Porcupine at 12.30 where we lunched & after marching about 4 or 5 miles went into camp on the bank of the Yellowstone; good camp. Marched —

Saturday—July 29, 1876. Broke camp at 5 am; took to the bluffs. Some hills about $2^1/_2$ miles from River are well timbered with pine— there is a similar cluster about 35 miles above the Big Horn on N. bank of Yellowstone. We crossed the Great Porcupine which is a running stream, pebbled bottom, 20 yds wide. About 5 miles further went into camp at foot of bottom, good camp, wood, 22 ½ miles.

Sunday. July 30. Broke camp at 5:15 a.m. & took to the bluffs again; at the foot of the bluffs is a very good spring, clear & cold. The day promises to be sultry & hot.

A good many of the 2nd Cav & 7th Infty are being taken sick on a/c of lack of vegetables. They require "anti-scorbutics." Was at Lt. Roe's last evening. Dr. Paulding told me there were 32 of 2nd Cav. sick since leaving Big Horn on 27th. When four or five miles from camp Corp'l Nolan came out to meet us. Also "Dr." Stein. Gibson[107] lunched with us today and after lunch we moved ahead & went into camp.

I went down to the boat to get my trunk but it could not be found. I got my tents, stoves, & things. It is quite an improvement on a Dog tent to have a place to stand up in while dressing. Corpl Nolan found my trunk & we are informed a mail will leave in half an hour. Surely not much time to write a letter.

July 31st. Laid about camp fixing up—have good healthy meals and <u>appetites</u> too.

End of first diary.

---

[107] Francis Marion Gibson (1847–1919) was 1st lieutenant of Company H under Benteen, who ordered Gibson to take the lead during the scout to the left on June 25 before the battle. He retired a captain in 1891 but was recalled to active service in 1918 during WWI.

END NOTES—FIRST DIARY

The first notes were obviously taken in the field and refer to observations Godfrey made while viewing the dead on the Custer battlefield.

Recognized
Stungewitz Co. C
Boston Custer[1]

===============

Marks

I saw 2 [marks]; Goddess of Liberty on left arm, eagle on right fore arm T.W.C.[2]

=============

Tho am but a [*unreadable*] boy as all Roman had stood and which in [*unreadable*] upon to [*unreadable*] that yet the [*unreadable*].

=============

The following notes are financial accounts. "Cr" indicates credit and "Dr" indicates draft.

July—Loaned Penwell $5.00

July [*illegible*] Mess		
Hare	Cr	13.40
Co. K	Dr	1.90
Godfrey	Cr	2.00
Hare	Cr	6.05
Hare	Cr	3.50
Hare	Cr	20.45

---

[1] Boston Custer (1848–June 25, 1876) was the youngest brother of General Custer and a civilian employee on the expedition. Ygnatz Stungewitz was a 29-year-old Russian immigrant and the clerk of Company C.
[2] Thomas Ward Custer.

Godfrey	Cr	1.00

==================

Mess [invoice?]	
~~16~~th 6 cans salmon	1.5
Beef	1.05
Tongue	.50
Chicken [?] H	5.00
~~Brockhorth~~[?]	40) 15.00 (39
Co. K to 2 ½ bu[shel?] Potatoes	1.9
Com[missary] Bill	13.40
Potatoes 15	24.00
Eggs 80/1200	1.50
Com[missary] Bill	(50) 20.45
" "	1.00

==================

Pat Coakley $1.00
Busnahan   1.00
Brown   1.00

==================

Ord. Circular NC02 '73
Price List
Calc .44 cost $18.00 per "M"

41

THE SECOND DIARY

Tuesday, August 1, 1876. About noon the Steamer *Carroll* came up with 6 Co's of the 22nd Infty, Lt. Col. Otis commd'g. Capts. Dickey, Clarke, Goodloe, Hooten, Poole, Lts. Conway, Kell, Casey, Dykman and others on board. After welcoming all we asked Goodloe, Kell, Casey & Dykman to dinner. Sent horses down for them. Burckhardt spread himself on the layout and we had a right sociable time of it.

In the evening went down to the 22nd camp & spent the eve with them. Got a lot of papers.

Wednesday. Aug. 2nd. After the troops were [paid; *corner of page torn*], I wrote a letter to [wife?], made out my pay [acct for July] and gave them to [Col.] Smith for delivery.

I saw General Forsyth[1] & apologized for not calling over to see him last night as I had gone to bed when I found out that he was in camp. Saw Genl Terry who told me that Larned had been appointed Prof. of D'g. He was mad & thot it was an outrage as we all think him a systematic shirk.[2] I took dinner with Mr. Cook, Colonel Cook's brother, Col. Reno, Benteen and Sim Boorleigh. After a pleasant time we left and the *Carroll* pulled out for Lincoln. As soon as [I came; *page torn*] to camp I learned that [*illegible*] two boats [*illegible*]. I rode down to [the river] & the boat with 5th Infty and Det. of 7th Cav. men who had been left at Lincoln in chg of property & sick were insight. They gave a big cheer pulled to the shore. I jumped on board & showed them where the landing was. Genl. Miles,[3] Capts Hathaway,[4] Carter,[5] Ovenshine[6] & others all old

---

[1] James William Forsyth (1834–1906) was a career officer with much experience on the staff of General Phil Sheridan during the Civil War and Indian Wars. He was commander of the 7th Cavalry during the Wounded Knee Massacre on December 29, 1890.

[2] Lt. Charles W. Larned had been with the 7th Cavalry on the 1873 Yellowstone Expedition. He was appointed Professor of Drawing at West Point on the very day that Custer died.

[3] Nelson Appleton Miles (1839–1925) served as a general in the Civil War, the Indian Wars, and the Spanish–American War. He was eventually Commanding General of the Army. He described Wounded Knee as "the most abominable criminal military blunder and a horrible massacre of

friends were on board. Mr. Garlington was on the *Josephine*. Carter, Baldwin & Garlington each had a "billet doux" from my darling. But she gave me heck for not writing oftener, & says Mrs. Moylan gets five letters to her one & she cried because mine was so short. It was the first letter for [two weeks] although I've sent her four or five; one by Ellis and one by Buford.

Aug. 3 Thursday. Looked over the papers sent by darling. Some severe criticisms emanate from the pens of many who know nothing of Indian warfare. They seem to think the same grand tactics are employed in it that is used in "civilized" warfare, or battles.

Capt. Carter took dinner with us. In the evening went fishing with Hare but did not catch anything. We went up to Head Qtrs. Sang the Star Spangled Banner with vim, Auld Lang Syne and Old Hundred.

Aug. 4, Friday. Wrote a letter to my darlings and issued ordnance. [*illegible*] boxed up our surplus to ship on *Durfee* to Lincoln. We also got some horses but many have the distemper and will probably give it to many of the old horses. Had several callers today. Went up to see about transportation and found we would have one wagon on the trip.

Aug. 5. Saturday. Burckhardt, Blunt, Foley & Murphy were discharged today to go down on the Steamer *E. H. Durfee*. I regret to loose [sic] all of them as they have been excellent soldiers. I finished my letter to mamma put it inside of my Diary which closes July 31st. I gave them to Blunt to carry "to Mrs. Godfrey."

---

women and children" (*A Hero to His Fighting Men*, DeMontravel, 1998). He was married to a niece of General William T. Sherman.

4 Forrest Henry Hathaway (1844–1923) was in Miles' 5th Infantry Regiment. He was a Civil War veteran, retired a brigadier general, and is buried with his wife at the Vancouver Barracks National Cemetery.

5 Probably Mason Carter (b. Cary Carter; 1834–1909). Initially enlisted in the navy at 14, he served in the army in the Civil War and Indian Wars, receiving a Medal of Honor for actions at Bear Paw Mountain in 1877 (*Military Times*).

6 Samuel Ovenshine (1843–1932) served in the Civil War and remained with the 5th Infantry afterwards. He led his brigade during the battles of Manila and Zapote Bridge in the Spanish American War. He received a Silver Star for his actions in these two battles.

We moved our camp a short distance preparatory to moving tomorrow. Have got Ackerman for cook.

Sunday Aug 6. The "General" sounded at 7 a.m. We packed, etc., to move across the river. The Regt. got across about 11 am. and we moved up the Rose Bud about 1 mile & went into camp. No shade within reach. We "skinned" down on baggage to comparative light marching order. We keep an "A" tent & fly also an A tent for a cook tent—My new cook. He hardly has the experience to resort to all the expedients necessary in the field—I take my cookstove. We will carry 5 days rations & 5 days forage (*unreadable in parentheses*). Capts. Carter, Hathaway, Hastings, Baldwin, Woodruff and [?] called a short time. We had a pleasant time. General Miles called but I was not in. I wrote to my loves—but the weather is too hot—98 in the shade.

Monday, Aug. 7th. We had mounted inspection at 8 am. I have 44 men in ranks; 1 teamster, 2 at Reg't Hdqars. 5 at Dept. Hdqtrs, Artillery & ordnance detachments—8 absent—47 serviceable horses present, 3 unserviceable; 3 on details; Finished my letter to my own, also wrote to the *Army and Navy Journal* correcting the prevailing mistake that Col. Benteen's column at the Battle of the Little Big Horn was a "Reserve" by design. Went down to the boat & got $1^1/_2$ lbs tea & posted my letter. Lieut. Macklin, 22d Infty & Lt. Whitten, 5th Infty. have been tried by [General Court Martial] for drunkenness. I am told the evidence is quite strong. Macklin receives a good deal of sympathy but Whitten none.

Tuesday Aug. 8, 1876. Reveille at 3 & moved promptly at 5 am, but it was 6:30 before the Rear Guard got out of camp or the wagon train crossed the creek. This has been a dreadful hot one—Several men had to be taken into the ambulances overcome by the heat.

In the afternoon about two o'clock heavy clouds appeared above the horizon from the direction of Big Horn Mts—This gave us a shadow about 1:30, and at 2 pm, we went into camp about 1 mile below our first camp out of Rose Bud June 22nd.

The odometer [on the wagon wheels] indicates 10 miles. We find the water running above and some very cold springs but the water is alkali.

A slight breeze sprang up in the evening but a lull during the night made us howl. The mosquitoes went for us. Mr. Garlington has changed his mess to Col. Benteen's—It was quite inconvenient to come so far for meals. A rumor spread that a man of C co. & his horse had been found both dead[7] but it seems some "Dough-boy" got it off as a joke. 9.84 m[ile]s.

Wednesday Aug. 9. Broke camp at 5. This morning is bracing but I have an almost unquenchable thirst. I drank nearly half a gal. of water yesterday—Am not going to do so today, so have kept a pebble in my mouth but it does not seem to excite the saliva.

I took two quinine pills and they help me. About 8:30 a.m. a light rain fell from the north. About 10 the sky was overcast and at 10:30 we have a "norther," so an overcoat feels comfortable. The scouts report Sioux. I feel as though I'd like to cuddle in a warm bed. A great deal of trouble with the road a number of crossings[,] a good many unnecessary & a great deal of unnecessary work. Marched 11 miles.

Thursday Aug. 10. Broke camp at 4:45 & marched in advance of the train; the sun rose clear and soon got warm. About 9 o'clock the Crows came in & reported Sioux ahead. We saw a very large smoke up the creek. After advancing about 1 mile we saw a heavy dust and the Crows put on their war paint—We saw persons approaching and immediately formed a skirmish line with the 2nd Cavalry deployed as skirmishers in our rear. Soon after Bill Cody, alias "Buffalo Bill," rode up to our line from Genl Crook's command which was about six miles above us and had gone into camp. Of course all the excitement as to Indians was over the alarm was given by the Indian scouts because they had seen the Shoshone scouts.

We rode ahead and went into camp just below Genl Crook's command. Met a good many officers of both Infty and Cav. Lt.

---

[7] Stories have persisted since the battle that perhaps a soldier escaped and died on the Rosebud.

Hayden DeLany, 9th Infty; Maj. Burt, 9th Infty; Jack Hayes, 5th Cav. We got orders to prepare to leave wagons and take 15 days rations. Marched 15 miles.

Friday, August 11. Ordered to take 15 days rations on 8 pack mules, no cooking utensils, no officers baggage except what they carry on their private horses. Only one blanket & overcoat per man. I drew rations with the company & for Hare, too. Carried one comforter & shelter tent on private horse. We left camp about 11:30—Some of the packs did not get out of camp for over an hour. The 5th Infty under Genl Miles went down then to the river last night & from there will go down to the mouth of Tongue per Steamer to head off the Indians if possible. He takes with him two (2) 3-inch rifles. The 22nd Infty had very much the experience we had when we started off with our pack train. We went directly across to Tongue River which [we] struck in about 11 miles, good road practicable for wagons, and camped on it. Marched 13 1/2 miles.

We had the Wolf Mts. to our right and Little Wolf Mts. on our front until we struck the Tongue. When we crossed the Tongue we came into an old Indian camp made since the Battle. It had been burnt off but some remnants of clothing were found showing them to be the same who were in the Battle. Some said they saw where some had been burnt at the stake, but I am told the indications by Indian interpretation said that had been some miners & over six mo[nths] ago. It began raining after we got into camp & continued all night. I saw Genl Crook, Lt. [sic] Bourke[8] and Scuyler[9] of his staff.

Saturday Aug. 12. I went down to 5th Cav Camp for a few moments when I heard the advance was moving out. So I hurried to join and found the 7th had taken the advance. I met Genls Merritt[10]

---

[8] Captain John Bourke was one of the most interesting men in the army at this time. Friend and adjutant to General George Crook, he was a scholar and later wrote the classic biography, *On the Border with Crook* (2015, BIG BYTE BOOKS).
[9] Walter S. Schuyler (1849–1932) was from New York and later retired there, a brigadier-general.
[10] General Wesley Merritt, a Civil War veteran and no friend of Custer's, served on the board of the Reno Court of Inquiry in 1879 that looked into

and Carleton,[11] Maj. Upham,[12] 5th Cav; Maj Mills,[13] 3rd Cav., Charles King,[14] '66, Forbush[15] & "<u>shit</u>" W. P. Hall,[16] '68. I find all don't obey the orders so literally as I did about rations, & that they carry a good many extras. It rained a good deal and must have been pretty hard on the "doboys." When we went into camp it was raining & continued all night. Hare & I went fishing and caught 2 two "cats"; one we ate & gave the other to our strikers [orderlies]. Most everybody is without shelter & I don't think anybody will get much sleep. Marched 13 miles.

Sunday Aug. 13. Broke camp at 7:30. It rained at times but was a good marching day. We passed two Indian camps yesterday they seem to be taking their time & have very few tepees but very large herds of ponies. We passed through three more camps today. The Tongue valley is a very fine one and the grazing is superb. Well wooded with ash and cotton-wood. Except by making cuts to the river a practicable road "is not." The river runs to bluffs on either side and the curves of the river leaves necks of land shaped something like a tongue; it is easily imagined that may be the origin of the name "Tongue" river.

Just a few miles from camp of today we came to a very wide valley made by two creeks coming in from opposite sides, indeed it seemed

---

charges of cowardice against Marcus Reno.

[11] Godfrey may be mistaken as the only general officer serving in the Indian Wars named Carleton was James Henry Carleton (1814–1873).

[12] John J. Upham (1844–1898) was breveted a major for actions at Gettysburg during the Civil War.

[13] Anson Mills (1834–1924) was a Civil War veteran and remained in service until 1893. He was an inventor and entrepreneur after his service. See *Anson Mills: the Civil War, the Sioux War, and Beyond* (2015, BIG BYTE BOOKS).

[14] Charles King (1844–1933) was an 1866 West Point graduate.

[15] William C. Forbush (1845–1906) was an 1868 West Point graduate.

[16] William Preble Hall (1848–1927) clearly knew Godfrey at West Point, as Godfrey graduated one year ahead of him. It's unknown if "shit" was Hall's West Point nickname. There is no record of a demerit for any conflict between the two men (email from Litts, westpoint.edu, 9/1/2021). Hall was a Medal of Honor recipient for an action in Colorado in 1879. He also served in the Spanish-American War, in the Philippines, and retired a brigadier general.

almost like coming to the Yellowstone valley. We made camp about 5 pm. Marched 24 ½ miles. Officer of the day.

Monday Aug. 14th. Broke camp at 7:30 & continued down Tongue river to Pumpkin Creek, where the trail took up it. After marching up it about four or five miles we went into camp. Very much to our disgust we are under Genl Gibbon again. Something must be wrong about Genl Terry that he cannot hold control of Cavalry & Infty without having merely <u>nominal</u> command.[17]

Marched 15 ¾ miles.

We found the grazing superb today on Tongue river and very good in places on Pumpkin Creek. We passed through two old Indian camps—one on P'n Cr'k.[18] A courier came from Genl Miles saying Indians had not crossed Yellowstone. One Co. at Tongue, two at Powder River and one on St. boat patrolling river. <u>The camps look quite old</u>. Marched 15 ¾ miles Powder River.

Tuesday, Aug. 15, '76. The trail leaves Pumpkin Crk and strikes east. The canteens were ordered filled in anticipation of no water to perhaps Powder river. Had dyspepsia last night and a diarrhoea this morning. The soldier's diet does not agree with me.

Marched <u>20 ¼</u>.

We have our hard bread fried in the Bacon fat, and our coffee & sugar make up the ration. The country over is quite <u>Bad</u> in places especially making the Powder River side down the creek. We struck the Powder divide about 10 and got to where we had a view of Powder valley about 11:30 and then began the descent.

A good many of the Infty "played out" and we had to carry them on our horses. It is simply an encouragement to straggle and somebody in their battalions is lax to permit it. Goodloe,[19] Campbell[20] and Kell,[21]

---

[17] Or it could be that, given his well-known nature, he was being polite to Gibbon by giving him the command. It's uncertain why Godfrey complains about being under Gibbon, a highly respected Civil War veteran.

[18] Pumpkin Creek.

[19] Archibald Henry Goodloe (1842–1899) was an 1865 graduate of West Point. He died after a long invalidism with Bright's Disease.

[20] William J. Campbell (?–1885) 1st lieutenant of K Company, 22nd Infantry.

22nd, Walker,[22] 17th, were visiting us—Goodloe said he gave a man a good <u>kicking</u>—took him out of ranks—for straggling today.

Walker says he has been detailed as personal Aid de Camp on the staff of Genl Terry, apparently for the purpose of carrying orders to the Commdg. officer of 7th Cav. Maj. Reno has been playing "ass" right along and is so taken up with his own importance that he thinks he can "snip" everybody and comment on the orders he receives from Genl Terry's Hdqrs and insult his staff, so there is not any one the personal staff on speaking terms. We find very fine grass on Powder river and the country burnt off in spots.

Powder River. *Wednesday, Aug. 16.* Broke camp at the usual hour and marched right behind the Infty or in their vicinity. Genl Terry and staff were riding by McDougall, Varnum and myself. I passed the time of day to some of the staff when Genl Terry stopped and waited for us to come up to shake hands. It was through his pure goodness of heart, but it appears to me a Genl ought to be a little harder to approach. He asked about "the Bloody 7th" as he termed it.

I understand that he has said if he had not so much respect for the officers of the Regt. he would put some other field officer on duty with the Regt. It seems that Reno's self-important rudeness makes him unbearable.

I was very sorry to learn that Goodloe, 22nd, had a paralytic stroke today and is helpless. It probably was induced by exposure. Poor fellow, he cannot speak but will very likely recover as he has some strength in his right side.

Had a talk with Doane,[23] 2nd Cav. tonight; he was at Goodloe's tepee constructing a mule litter. I think I'll suggest to Genl Terry to

---

[21] William H. Kell (1842–1916) served as a soldier under his father, Colonel John Kell (KIA), in the Civil War. The son later served in the Spanish-American War and in the Philippines. He died suddenly of heart disease.

[22] Henry P. Walker had served at Fort Abraham Lincoln the previous year under Major General Thomas Leonidas Crittenden (1819–1893), whose son, Lt. John Jordan Crittenden, joined the 7th Cavalry just before its departure to destiny in May 1876. John Crittenden died with Custer and was identified by the broken pieces of his glass eye.

put Doane in command of the scouts, for he certainly has a great deal of "Savez" about Indian character—is experienced in plain-craft and a man of good judgment and very observing. We are camped opposite our old camp of 8th to 11th of June. Marched 19 miles.

Powder River. *Thursday Aug. 17th.* Broke camp at the usual about 7 am—Genl Crook's Infty. leaves every morning at 5 am and get into camp at or before the cavalry do; and their marches are independent of each other. While ours leave at the same time we do and we have a Battalion tagging after them as escort and they don't get the benefit of the cool of the morning.

We marched down the Powder valley and struck across to our old wagon trail and followed that, making our march a good deal longer than necessary. Part of the country has been burnt off. A good suggestion was made today that all the country be burnt off entirely from the Little Missouri west & north to the British line. The Buffaloe [sic] will not roam where the country has been burnt off and the Indians must go to the Buffaloe—Therefore we would drive off the Indians.

Met "Philo" Clark,[24] 2nd Cav., who came down from Ellis[25] by boats to join his Regt. He has been Adjt. of his Regt. We have camped on the Powder about $1^1/_2$ miles from Yellowstone. Marched 23.

Powder River. *Friday, Aug. 18.* Went down to see about rations. Col. Smith, A.A.A.G. told me we would in all probability draw rations from [Fort] Lincoln the next issue unless of course the [Indian] trail should cross the Yellowstone [towards Canada]. I remarked that it would suit me and he said it he thought it would most everybody else too.

---

23 Gustavus Cheyney Doane (1840–1892) was a Civil War veteran, explorer, inventor, and entrepreneur. Doane played a major role in designing litters to carry the wounded survivors of the Little Bighorn disaster to the steamboat *Far West* on the Bighorn River.
24 William Philo Clark (1845–1884) was the preeminent expert in Indian sign language and wrote the book on it. See *The Indian Sign Language* (2015, BIG BYTE BOOKS).
25 Fort Ellis (1867–1886) was near Bozeman, MT.

The P.T. [Post Trader] sold nearly everything out—tobacco & such things at outrageous prices. We have prepared to move tomorrow. I went over to 2nd Cav. camp at Capt. Ball[26] invitation to get our onions. Their hospitality was bountiful. We were given eggs, potatoes & onions by Ball, and Doane gave me one can of Pine Apples, one can of Preserves. They got a lot of vegetables by boat from Ellis and shared with everybody. Schofield laid out a big cake.

Mo[uth]. Powder River, M.T. *Saturday, Aug. 19.* We did not move as we expected with our 14 days rations towards Lincoln and those whom we love. So far no evidence appears that they [the Sioux and Cheyenne] have crossed the river. The Plan now seems to be for all to follow trail toward Lincoln and if necessary Crook can get rations there or from there.[27] The wagon train to go down to Buford[28] and from there march down the Mo [Missouri River]. The Montana trains wait for Montana Troops.

The steamboat has been ordered to Rose Bud for all supplies, etc. at Depot. We had Lloyd[29] and Robertson,[30] Infty, Hare classmates for Breakfast. We felt happy to dispense a hospitality on vegetables.

We laid in some more stores from the Sutlers store. The Com. Dept. fails to furnish any stores for sale to officers; a plain case of neglect on somebody's part.

Sunday, Aug. 20. Genl Crook cannot move until his Infty gets shoes, so we must wait for the St[eam] boat to come down. We

---

[26] Edward Ball (?–1884) was a Civil War veteran.
[27] Crooks command was about to begin what would become known as the Starvation March or Horsemeat March. Before they reached Deadwood, SD, the soldiers would be out of supplies and living on horsemeat.
[28] Fort Buford (1866–1896) was at the confluence of the Yellowstone and Missouri Rivers.
[29] Charles F. Lloyd (1851–1924) graduated with Luther Hare from West Point in 1874 and was serving in the 14th Infantry in 1876. He served in the Spanish-American War and was a U.S. Marshall. He left the army in 1883 and became a Montana rancher. He retired a colonel.
[30] Edgar Brooks Robertson (1852–1924) was in the 9th Infantry in 1876. He later served in the Spanish-American War, the Boxer Rebellion, and the Philippines, retiring a colonel.

passed the day sociably a good many visitors from the other camps. Wrote to my darlings.

Powder River. *Monday Aug. 21.* Word comes up from the St. boat *Carroll* that a mail is on board and the Indians are at Standing Rock. Also [they] have been firing into boats on the Missouri. That a cantonment of ten Cos of Infty will be formed at mouth of Tongue River. Got a mail today; two letters from my darlings at Lincoln, one from father. Mage Rice, Col. Barnitz[31] [residence 1761 Cedar avenue Cleveland Ohio; *brackets in original*]. Lt. R[*unreadable*], Ex Sergt Courtland Morris,[32] Ex-Blacksmith W. S. Harvey, one from Sergt. Winney's brother, Scuylerville, Utica Co N.Y. and mothers brother[33] Lorain, Lorain Co., Ohio—also papers.

I see father had my letter to Mary published as he said he had so many inquiries to read it. I wish he had taken some care to have had the construction of sentences made more perfect. It was written hurriedly while everything pertaining to refitting company was on my mind and a thousand details to attend to. I see when mention is made of other officers it has been omitted.

Went over to the train today to get some articles out of wagon & saw Hughes[34] who says we will take 42 wagons & ambulances with us to carry extra forage & rations should they be needed.

Tuesday, Aug. 22. Met Capt. Mills & Lt. Sibley,[35] 2nd Cav. We were caught in the rain while at the Commissary buying stores and had a disagreeable time getting home.

---

[31] Captain Albert Barnitz (1835-1912) was badly wounded in November 1868 at the Battle of Washita.

[32] Courtland L. Morris (1846–1924) had served in Company K of the 7th Cavalry.

[33] Matthew A. Chambers (1827–1901) was, at the time Godfrey wrote, his mother's only living brother.

[34] Robert Patterson Hughes (1839–1909) was a Civil War veteran, as well as aide-de-camp to his brother-in-law, General Alfred Terry. Hughes served in the Philippines during the Spanish-American War and the Philippine War.

[35] Frederick William Sibley (1852–1918), was a career Army officer, and graduate of the West Point class of 1874, who served in the U.S. Cavalry for 42 years. He became famous for the "Sibley Scout" during Crook's layover on Goose Creek after the Battle of the Rosebud.

Wednesday Aug. 23. Mouth Powder River, M.T. I went over the river to get canvass for men & some commissaries. I got my trunk, looked at my darlings' pictures; got my razor & housewife[36] to carry on the trip and asked Dr. Harvey to attend to it and deliver to Mrs. Godfrey at Lincoln; saw Goodloe who has improved so he can sit up asked him to go to my house at Lincoln. He cannot speak; his right side is paralyzed.

I left camp without my coat it was so warm & pleasant, but it clouded up and began to rain & kept it up all night; very cold & wind blowing hard. Poor men & animals. The dog tents do not afford a great deal of protection against a blowing rain. I wrote all evening to my loves at Lincoln. The St. *Far West* coming down.

Mouth of Powder River. *Thursday Aug. 24.* Lay in bed till 9 am; rain still continues and the Powder River is up so we cannot cross over it. We have not had any forage yet although the other commands have had. I wrote to Mary till breakfast was ready. Today is Hare's birthday (25th).

I started down to Steamboat landing but boat pulled away before I got to it—so I put in time writing to Mary & writing this. Orders have been issued for all dismounted men to be sent down on boat. Returned to boat at 5 pm got some cigars out of my trunk and asked Dr. Clark & Grant Marsh[37] to please send trunk down to Lincoln by *Carroll* and gave Dr. Clark a letter containing money & key to trunk addressed to Mrs. Godfrey. Hope all will get through safely. Went to bed early. Marched on off[icer of the] Day ~~and visited guard just before Reveille~~.

Friday Aug. 25, 1876. Visited guard just before reveille. Broke camp at 6; tried two or three fords but none seemed to be fordable.

---

[36] A small case for needles, thread, and other small sewing items (Oxford Languages).

[37] Grant Marsh (1834–1916) was a legendary steamboat captain. In the summer of 1876, he supplied and transported the command via the steamboat *Far West*. After the Battle of the Little Bighorn, Marsh made a record-breaking dash down three rivers to take the wounded survivors back to Fort Lincoln. See *Conquest of the Missouri* (2019, BIG BYTE BOOKS).

We found the ground very damp so it ~~weakens~~ exhausts the horses very materially to march. Marched up Powder River about 7 miles on west side and forded the river. Was a little above belly deep [to a horse]. Packs came through O.K. The ford led to where the Indian village had been about three weeks before. We took the trail which led to the top of a very wide Plateau and over it. We crossed and kept on up the river to a small creek with water from recent rains and went into camp. As we came up river we saw Crook's column moving out—and when we reached the plateau we met Genls Terry & Gibbon with Infty & wagon train. Soon after we went into camp, a courier [from?] Buffaloe Bill came to ~~camp~~ Genl Terry with dispatches that Steamer *Josephine*, with Col. Whistler,[38] 22nd Infty, was coming up river with further supplies for cantonment. Also some mail was sent up *but I did not get any* nor did Moylan or Gibson. Everybody else got letters from their wives. Genl Terry took French's company and moved up to Crook's camp about 10 miles up the river. Marched about 17-1/2 miles.

Saturday Aug. 26th Marched $22^1/_2$ miles. Broke camp 7:30 am and turned back to Yellowstone. Considerable trouble with B & M company packs. [I] am rear guard of cav. At 10:30 am received orders to send co. packs & cooks ahead with Regt and take rear guard of Everything, whole column. Shot two abandoned horses left by other cos.

We found an excellent road over the Plateau from Powder to O'Fallons Creek, and a very good place for wagons to come down directly on the Point bluffs at junction of two rivers. And a splendid view of the country both up and down the river.

Got into camp at 3:30 p.m. Gen Crook's command marched down to [*unreadable*; see note[39]] hoping to [find?] Indians.

Mouth of O'Fallons Creek, Yellowstone. *Sunday Aug 27.* Broke camp at 7 a.m. and marched down stream (crossed O'Fallons Creek)

---

[38] Joseph Nelson Garland Whistler (1822–1899) was a career Army officer, and a veteran of the Mexican War and the Civil War.
[39] Bourke wrote in *On the Border with Crook* that they headed toward the Little Missouri on this day.

about four miles when we were ferried across Yellowstone by steamers *Carroll* and *Yellowstone*. Col Reno had it official that 5th and 22nd Infty and our Regts of cavalry other than 7th Cav would be designated to form cantonment at Mo [mouth] of Tongue River.[40] That we would not be kept out later than Oct 15. The probabilities[41] being that we would go in right away.

Weston was on Board and said Mrs. Godfrey had given my mail to Ball and Ball returned Lincoln. Pshans! She ought to have known better than to have trusted him. Benteen and I went fishing. He told me he had the detail of Recruiting. I am glad he gets it over Every body else besides my self—as he certainly is entitled to it over Every body else.

The Regt will certainly feel his loss very much for some two years. We got across the river by 5:30 but right away moved at 6:40. The Infty a little before. The Commissary had some cans of beef (meats) and some heifers were killed after we crossed. The cans were not proportioned, so some men got some & others more. Only a small part of the beef was issued. We marched rapidly for about 6 ¼ miles and bivouacked without water. Total march 11 ½.

Monday Aug 28th. We broke camp at 5 a.m. Marched 5 miles & we found water. Bivouacked & had breakfast. At 9:30 we moved again. Soon after we left a big fire broke out in camp. We came up a very pretty valley where we camped; was a fine spring. After marching some distance we began to prospect for water and went over to the creek valley we had been marching over & which was to our left, when we found water in pools but evidently fed by springs. Plenty of wood and a very pretty camp—Buffaloe were seen & killed by scouts. Marched 20.96.

Thursday Aug. 29, 1876. Broke camp at 6 am. Was in advance of Regt. Continued up creek valley Xed the divide about 10. Hare and McDougall went hunting; we saw a good many Antelope and after

---

[40] General Nelson Miles was in command of the 5th Infantry. He established Cantonment Tongue River, which later became Fort Keogh, named for Myles Keogh who died with Custer.

[41] The wording here is difficult to decipher in the diary.

we crossed the divide a herd of buffaloe was seen. On reaching the creek valley we grazed our horses and soon after a buffaloe herd was seen coming over the bluffs. A detail of two was made from each company. I got on the pony and we started for the herd. I could not make the pony go fast enough and so did not get a shot and went on over the hills. Pvt Robert was with, we soon found a herd on the top and it would be a good idea to drive it toward the column. We drove it about two miles and found the column had stopped halted. So we pitched into the herd. I got an old bull cut out and he showed fight; Pony understood the game and I rode up pretty near and gave the old fellow a shot; he ducked his head but I gave him no opportunity for a rush and soon let him come up alongside and gave him one through the belly which he didn't like & ducked for another rush. Still I gave him no opportunity and let him come up alongside again when I shot him in the spine and down his hind qtrs went. He made a desperate attempt to recover himself and fell. Soon after another herd came up and I thought I'd take a cow. I got up along side and missed. I found only one more shot in my pistol & so withdrew from the contest; The pony did not like to give up. I went back to the bull, took out the loin, hump, & "dornicks"[42] and a hind quarter—a great many buffaloe were killed & the command supplied with fresh meat; the first for a long time (10 days). We halted after going down the valley sometime where there was some muddy water, dug holes and got good water; the Cav made coffee; the Infty continued the march to Pool water (spring) about three miles below. We had to use buffaloe chips for fuel. We moved on after coffee to camp below the Infty. Today was the first time buffaloe hunting ever gave me any sporting excitement. Marched 17.62 miles.

Wednesday Aug. 30. Left camp at 6:30 am. Marched about 1 mile & waited until nearly 8 am for the Infty packs to move out of column. We kept an easterly direction over the divide. Passed several good water holes. Marched to a creek said to empty opposite Glendive crk. Here Buffaloe Bill and Herndon scouts who had been sent to Glendive on 28th, rejoined us—no news from the river. As soon as we struck water Genl Gibbon said his Infty could not march

---

[42] Godfrey is probably referring to the testicles.

<u>any farther</u>. We were two miles above wood and good camping ground. I went down with packs to get wood. Marched 17^1/$_2$ miles.

The day was not very warm either. Towards evening it got cloudy & cool. There was no excuse why Infty could not march any farther. Three horses were abandoned by the command.

Thursday, Aug. 31. Reveille at the usual hour. The 2nd Cav. pickets reported three (3) horsemen as having passed near camp. The scouts were sent out & found that three (3) antelope had passed them. At 8:15 we left camp. The Infty & Genl Terry with 2 Cav. continued on down the creek and we moved east across the divide. The country was pretty rough but we had an ambulance and a practicable road could be found for a wagon train. We crossed several streams of good water and saw plenty of antelope & deer and went into camp on a running creek, had some difficulty getting to the valley which might have been avoided by going "lower down" or "higher up."

Just as we were going down from the divide, I saw the smoke of St. boat and after putting Co. in camp I got on pony, took Trumptr Penwell[43] and started for the river—I went to a point but could not see anything of her so didn't get a mail. Marched about 20 miles.

Yellowstone River. *Friday Sept. 1.* Broke camp at 7 am and kept on our easterly direction crossed a creek of running water about 12 miles out and continued toward river & finally struck the bottom in which we found a very good camping place, but Col. Reno thought he ought to go farther and we marched about three miles, but we found the country all burnt off, so we made a bad camp. When about two miles from camp we heard a St. boat. Wallace & I with a detail went over to it; we found it after a good deal of hard work, riding through underbrush, sloughs, etc.; it was the *Carroll*, but had no mail for us and was loaded with machinery for the new Post at Tongue River. After we got into camp scouts were sent to the Mo. [Missouri] river to look for "signs" and to Genl Terry with a report of

---

[43] George B. Penwell (1849–1905) was trumpeter of Godfrey's company. He attended the 1886 10th Anniversary reunion at the battlefield.

the scout. The *Yellowstone* came up afterwards and we got some forage off her. No mail. Marched about 18 miles.

Camp on Yellowstone. *Saturday, Sept. 2, 1876.* The scouts came to camp at 6:30 from the Mo. and reported "no signs" and the country all burnt off to the Mo. We broke camp at 8 and got into camp at 12:30 having marched about 15 miles up the Yellowstone Valley. We had a good camp. The *Silver Lake* was aground, and the *Carroll* and *Yellowstone* came up. We took 13 horses & 50 head of cattle from them to lighten their loads. They remained all night. The *Josephine* and *Benton* passed down. Had a visit from Col. Reno, Lts. Wagner[44] and Low, Lt. Jacobs 6th Inf. on *Silver Lake*. Capt. [Thomas] Britton, 6th Infty, gave us a lot of a head of cabbage and some onions to each mess. Hare killed a Prairie Chicken & we had a royal feast for supper.

Dr. Lawrence gave me a paper bag full of flour from his St. boat *Yellowstone*. Made requisitions for tobacco, and made the men's hearts glad, as they were out. Marched about [...].

Glendive Creek. *Sunday Sept. 3.* Left camp about 9 am and got to Glendive where the troops were camped about 1:30. Was Rear Guard and had the cattle to guard which delayed me somewhat as they were not used to travelling and the day was warm. Gave my application for "L" to Col. Reno.

Opp. Glendive M.T. *Monday Sept. 4th.* Remained in camp. Gave my application to Col. Reno who endorsed it. My application stated that Capt. Sheridan[45] was absent on detail & Braden absent sick. Col. Reno forwarded the application approved & earnestly recommended "The facts as stated by Lt. Godfrey will leave the Co. without an officer for some time & the 2nd Lt. is probably inexperienced"—and took the application to Capt. Smith in person & spoke to Genl Terry in person. Had a slight touch of headache.

---

[44] John C. Waggoner (1836–1899) was a packer with the pack train.
[45] Michael Vincent Sheridan (1840–1918) was at this time on detached detail as aide-de-camp for his famous brother, Phil Sheridan. M.V. Sheridan was detailed with troopers the following summer to retrieve the remains of the officers on the LBH battlefield.

The expedition has "busted" and now preparations are being made for the several troops & columns. The 22nd continue here as guard for a [indecipherable] depot—and the 5 Infty go to Tongue river for cantonment. The 7th Infty & 2nd Cav. go to Montana & the 6th Inft & 7 Cav. go to [Fort] Buford and from there we will go home.

Tuesday Sept. 5. Made calls on officers of other Regts. Saw Col. Reno about making a change of Non Comm Officers in Co. He would not issue any order but I issued an order making Corpl Murray,[46] 1st Sergt. [moved?] Sergt Rott[47] to Sergt and made Rachael[48] Corpl— which I think will be an improvement on the old regime. Sergt. Rott was too careless about the comfort of the men and seldom said anything about matters I ought to have known about. The rations got short and no steps were taken to inform me so it could be rectified. Murray has been a Non Comm Off eleven years & so I had to jump Corpl Nolan[49] who is a good man but I guess he is philosophical enough to understand.

Col. Reno told me I had better see Genl Terry about my transfer which I did in the evening, who told me it was all right and approved and would be forwarded first mail. All the officers of the expedition collected at Dept Hdqrs in the evening where we remained about two hours singing. We parted with Auld Lang Syne and L.M. Doxology, Praise God etc. and general hand shaking.

Wednesday Sept. 6th. Got up at 6:30, ate breakfast and went to the St. boat. Keeven[50] came to the tent to sell his mare, a little beauty. Hare bought her for $125 and gave an order on Capt. Harmon for the am't—which I endorsed.

---

[46] The only Murray in the roster was Thomas Murray (1836–1888), an Irish immigrant who was sergeant of Company B. He was wounded in the hilltop fight and later received a Medal of Honor.

[47] Louis Rott (184?–?) was a recent German immigrant, having only arrived in America in 1870.

[48] Henry W. Raichel (1847–1877) died the following year at the Battle of Bear Paw Mountain.

[49] John Nolan (1838–1893) was an Irish immigrant but on detached duty during the battle.

[50] This may have been Michael Keegan (1846–1900) an Irish immigrant.

I wrote a short note to my own and endorsed my order on Brooks Bros. for a blouse & pants so as to have something decent to wear when I get in. The 6th Foot [infantry] pulled out at 8 and we followed about 9:30. The 2nd Cav. pulled out at the same time. They have about twenty four or five days march before them. We will probably consume as much time, as we must use up ten days rations before we go in to Buford ~ 80 miles down the river. We made camp at 12:00 having marched about ten miles.

Hare killed an antelope and a Mule Eared deer. I've felt badly all afternoon.

Thursday, Sept. 7th. Broke camp at 7 and marched down the river and went into camp where we overtook the *Silver Lake* aground. Nothing noteworthy took place—except our camp we left in the morning took fire and made a heavy smoke—which fire is very unfortunate as the Infty will have to transport supplies from Buford for the cantonments. After getting in camp I took Sergt. Hose[51] and one man to go hunting. We met Mr. O'Kelley[52] "*Herald* Correspondent," who with Lt. Hare had been hunting. They got nothing & Mr. O'Kelley went with us. We went down to the river saw where a very large bear had crossed a slough and we tried to cross but it was too boggy, and we continued our hunt to the bluffs but returned with nothing. It turned cold and rained by dark.

Friday Sept. 8th. It continued raining more or less this morning till 10 o'clock. About 8 a.m. the steamer *Far West* came up and had a mail. Everybody got mail but me. *Why?* Why have I not heard anything since in July from my family. It makes me feel bitter, mad, not even a [news]paper did I get. Moylan had a letter from his wife, so it can't be they are sick or she would have mentioned it—We broke camp at 4 pm. and marched about <u>7 miles</u> and went into camp on a creek, wooded with elm. Excellent grass and water. Had my mind whirling tonight on plans for "campaigning" after getting to Lincoln. Continues cold and raw.

---

[51] George Hose (1850–1924) was a German immigrant.
[52] James Joseph O'Kelly (1845–1916) was an Irish nationalist journalist and politician who in 1876 was writing for the *New York Herald*.

Saturday Sept. 9. Broke camp at 7:15 am and continued our march down the river. The pack mules are playing out, getting weak, and will soon give up the load for the "Cavelyard." got into camp about 11 am. Passed the Steamer *Carroll* on her way up the river— No mail—Went into camp near banks of Y.S. [Yellowstone River] no grass, difficult to get water. The Y.S. here partakes of the character of the Mo.—cut banks and no pebbles, sand bars become a feature of the river. Tortuous channel—Marched 16 miles.

Sunday Sept. 10th The 1st Battalion was ordered to march back to a point 20 miles up the River. The St. *Josephine* came up about 6:30 am with supplies for Glendive and was ordered to put out forage at both camps and it turned out that Maj. Reno had been ordered to have one Batt. at that point and to march the other to a point not more than 25 miles to Buford and from these two points scout the river—so the Capt. of the boat, mentioning that he was to put out forage at <u>both</u> camps, and asking where the other was, made Col. Reno nervous, so our Batt. was ordered saddled. After we got saddled & packed, some couriers arrived from Buford directing the forces to "Wolf Point" Assiniboine Agcy on the Mo. River, where it seems they have a report that Indians are crossing or have crossed. So we unpacked, unsaddled to wait for something else and broke camp at 11 am. About ten (10) miles from camp N.W. we crossed a creek which had cut off the fire and found good grass & water, plenty of dry wood—our march was continued about ten or twelve miles farther and we camped in a very pretty cove, the head of the stream we crossed 12 miles below—and near two pointed buttes (adjacent) we found plenty of wood, good grass; & water about one mile below the buttes. Evidences of trappers having been there at some recent year. Got cool in the evening & cloudy. Infty made good time. 22 miles.

Monday Sept. 11, 1876. The weather was cloudy & misty the fogs cut off the view of the country so it was almost impossible to keep the direction of compass. We crossed the "<u>divide</u>," the "<u>great divide</u>" about 9:30, and we stopped a short time, built fires & dried out a little. It began to be a question of a camp again as 'twas last night for when we could find wood was no water and when we found water no wood was to be seen. So we pursued our journey for about 25 miles and went into camp on wood—for fires we must have—and Mrs [Godfrey means "Misters"] Hare & Mathey[53] found water about ¾ miles below camp. It continued to rain all night; we had a big fire in front of the tent. We were ordered to make the rations last to include the 17[th,], Two days addition, so it gave us about 2/3 rations. This is done in anticipation of "no boat" when we reach the river and have to march down to Buford. The Comdg Officer [Reno] will not allow hunting for the present, so it will come pretty hard on the men. Nearly all the officers messes are out of provisions owing to the incompetency of Lt. Thompson, A.C.S. of Expedition. No officers stores are for sale & when we send up for parts of rations we are informed they cannot be had—and no flour.[54]

Tuesday, Sept. 12. Missouri Mouth of—Still raining & foggy; dismal & uncomfortable. About 9:30 we struck Bad Lands—and when the fog lifted the Mo. River was in sight about five miles from B.L. [Bad Lands] we had a very difficult place to descend. The Rear Guard had a very difficult time to get the ambulances down and were on the point of abandoning them; but finally got them down and broke one, so it had to be abandoned on the bank of the River, left for the boat to pick up. After the ambulances got in we were informed the comnd would move in two hours, and at 5:30 p.m. we marched up the River, until about 7:30 when we went into camp for the night, called by some Redwood Creek but from the map looks like Elk Prairie Creek—a stream of about ten yards wide—Have had a painful diarhoea for the past two days. Marched about 25 miles.

Camp near Mo. River 3 miles from Wolf Point Assinoboine Agency.

Wednesday Sept 13 Broke camp at 5 a.m. and continued the march up the River—was Rear Guard. Felt badly all day from my

---

[53] Edward Gustave Mathey (1837–1915) was 1st lieutenant of M Company. A French immigrant, Mathey served in the infantry throughout the Civil War.
[54] Douglas Scott, former chief archaeologist at the Little Bighorn National Monument, wrote that, while today we think of taking young boys and making men out of them, the frontier army took healthy young men and made physical wrecks out of them. Poor diet, injuries, and exposure took a terrible toll.

diarhoea bloody, mucous discharges. We got to this point about 10 o'clock—No boat in sight. Col. Reno, Wallace, & Hare, with an escort went to the Agcy which is located on the Left bank of the Mo. Lone Dog with a few families, passed on his way north six days ago, but no force of Indians have ~~done much~~ gone this way—and few have been into Fort Peck. Marched about 16 miles.

Hare got a few potatoes for distribution to the officers—There are no stores for sale at the Agcy and so we are compelled to wait for the boat for supplies and 10-to-1 there will not be any officer's stores on board. Lt. Jacobs and Mr. Leighton were at the Agcy—The boat left Buford yesterday p.m. and will probably be here by Friday—The Indians killed two Buffaloes today—<u>Old Bulls</u>.

The Agcy Indians are said to be out killing Buffaloe of which there are said to be many a few miles out from the River.

Camp on Mo. River. *Thursday Sept. 14* Moved camp about two miles to banks of river; fine camp, good grass, plenty of wood but difficult to get at water—My diarrhoea continues. Am officer of the day. After leaving our camp it was discovered to be on fire and I was sent back to find out where it originated & if it could be put out. I reported it originated in "A" Co. and it could be put out. The 1st Battln was ordered back to extinguish it (on foot). Moylan fixed the origin of the fire on Sergt Culbertson[55] of his Co. and reduced him to the ranks for his carelessness.

A slight frost last night.

Camp on N side of Mo River. *Friday Sept 15* Sent out several hunting parties this am. The Steamer *Chambers* came up about 12 p.m. and the "General" was sounded and we were soon crossing over the river by 5 p.m. Everything was crossed over and we went into camp. It was intended to move a few miles down the river but a few drinks put that out of mind and we concluded to have a sing.

---

[55] Ferdinand A. Culbertson is best known for having recovered a 7th Cavalry guidon while on burial detail at the battlefield (one of five the regiment carried). From 1895 to 2010, the guidon was owned by the Detroit Institute of Arts. It was auctioned by Sotheby's in 2010 for $2,210,500, including buyer's premium. The hammer price was $1.9 million.

[Sentence too faded to read] Col. Smith and Reno told me the matter of my going to "L" Co. would be fixed by having me temporarily assigned to "L" before we got in. Got some com. stores and a sack of potatoes from the Agcy.

Camp on Mo. River, M.T. *Saturday Sept 16.* Broke camp at 5:30 am. and marched 17 miles to Frenchman's fork, a pebbled stream about ten yards wide and went into camp for 3 hours to noon, got dinner. We marched at 1 p.m. across the Big Bend of the Mo. and camped at 4:30, distance 13 miles. Total distance 30 miles. Edgerly came up on a St. boat and bro't my mail.[56]

Sunday, Sept, 17 Broke camp at [*unreadable* but probably five]. Marched to the "Big Muddy," a stream which deserves its name, and nooned. The contractors are hauling & cutting hay for Fort Buford, a distance of about 32 miles from Buford—here we found but little wood. Constant camping at the crossing of so many parties uses up all the fuel, and the Buffaloe do not range this far down.

After nooning we continued our march to the "Little Muddy," which is a <u>clear</u> stream. We got to camp about dark and had considerable difficulty getting wood.

McDougall & Edgerly went to Buford last night. McDougall's mother and sister died (on the same day), and Mc expects to go to telegraph communication to learn of his father's doings. Edgerly goes down to draw supplies.

Monday Sept. 18 Marched to Fort Buford by 10:30 a.m. Tis called 15 miles. The road thro bottom is pretty bad and thro willows.

We passed the remains of old "Fort Union" once occupied by the <u>North Western</u> Fur Company—nothing but stones out of which the chimneys were built, wells, sinks etc. The Indian scout's qrs are comfortable looking log huts, one of which was octagonal and slides sloping and covered with dirt. The Entrance was on top and was sheltered at the entrance by a basket frame over which they fasten a

---

[56] About 4/5 of the page that Godfrey marked as "68" is too faded to decipher. Even inverting the page colors and adjusting for contrast and brightness fails to make the page readable. Page 69 starts with the September 17 entry.

skin. They were surrounded by the [Indian] loafers, painted, and as usual smoking. Some of the squaws & children were dressed in callico [sic] dresses. We passed by the fort and unsaddled about a half a mile away. We turned over our pack mules & have two wagons to the Regt. from here to Stevenson—leave here with two day's supplies. The Post looked clean and neat. I went to the store, bought a coffee mill, and looked thro the mail for a letter but didn't get anything. Saw Lt. Jacobs, Wagner, and "Lufo." No other officers called at camp nor showed any hospitality whatever to my knowledge. I presume their hospitality has been sorely taxed this summer by the numerous officers passing up & down the river and awaiting transportation. Still they were "Coffee Coolers." and we "warriors." We probably were not fit subjects to introduce into their families. Nearly all the officers took dinner at the store with Mr. Jordan.[57] After dinner I went in to pay my respects to Mrs. Jordan the first white lady I have seen in four (4) months. Genl Hazen[58] commands the post at present. After getting supplies we moved down on to a small creek about four miles out and camped.

Dry Camp *Tuesday Sept. 19th.* We marched to a creek four miles above the Muddy camped for noon and then moved to the "Muddy" and camped till nearly sundown. We fed, watered, cooked supplies and marched about 8 miles and went into a Dry camp.

Wednesday Sept. 20. Reveille at 5. Moved at 5:45 Col. Weir brought some wood and officers made coffee at his fire. We continued our march to "Tobacco Garden," a creek with wood in ravines and pretty good water. Met quite a number of Indians going out to their fall hunt. Didn't learn to what tribe they belonged; some of them were in wagons driving their teams and look quite accustomed to it. They still wore their Indian costumes—and looked quite gay. We met also a wagon train going to Tongue river post to the employees of wood contractor were with them. After nooning we continued our march to Grinnell[?] Point, a wood yard where we got

---

[57] Walter Booth Jordan (1847–1924) was the post trader at Buford along with his partner and brother-in-law, Joseph Leighton. Mrs. Jordan was the former Mary Emily Leighton.
[58] William Babcock Hazen (1830–1887) was a career Army officer who had risen to Corps command during the Civil War.

two day's rations but they didn't put off any bacon. So will go two days without the meat ration.

Sully's Lake, *Thursday Sept. 21*. Marched to Knife river and lunched for two hours. Distance marched 17 miles, and then to Sully's Lake. We crossed Shell creek. No wood and got to this place after dark. Slept badly on a/c of eating a late supper. Total distance 41 miles.

Fort Berthold[59] D.T. *Friday, Sept. 22*. Marched to this place 32 miles. We passed thro quite an extensively cultivated bottom—of corn principally, but had beans, squashes and potatoes. The village is made of logs and adobe and dirt covered structures. I could not make a minute inspection or even a satisfactory glance. The Agent, Mr. Darling,[60] informed me that they raised about 10,000 bushels of corn, fifteen or twenty thousand bushels of potatoes and that he had an appropriation of $12,000 with which to carry on the agency. Heretofore Mr. Tappan[61] has been the Agent and had an appropriation of some $60,000. How or where it was spent is another thing. We went to the Agcy boarding house & got a pitcher of fresh milk which we finished and sauntered at the Agents office till supper time and we took a square meal and settled for it with the agent, 50 cts each. He was not proprietor of the house, only a boarder.

Fort Stevenson,[62] D.T. *Saturday, Sept. 23*. Camped about a mile above Stevenson on a creek and went into the post. Met Col. Dan Huston,[63] Lts. Wetheral, Thompson and Dr Harvey. The Dr. has grown stouter and looks well. I took a bath and shave and after the column moved thro the Post, sent all stragglers to the command and

---

[59] The site of Fort Berthold is submerged under Lake Sakakawea in the 21st century.
[60] Charles W. Darling.
[61] John E. Tappan.
[62] Fort Stevenson (1867–1883) featured heavily in the memoir by its commander, Major General Régis de Trobriand, a French immigrant and distinguished Civil War veteran. See *Army Life in Dakota* (2016, BIG BYTE BOOKS).
[63] Daniel Huston Jr. (1824–1884) was a career soldier, Civil War veteran, and in command of Fort Stevenson in 1876.

then went to the qrs of Lt. Wetheral where we had considerable amusement singing; some got too tight to be amusing. Lt. Wetheral's qrs are neatly furnished the walls decorated with old engravings from the "Old Masters." After prancing some time we went to Dr. Harvey's for dinner and had a very good spread to which we did ample justice and washed it down with Sherry wine, after which we had our desert of champagne & coffee. Gibson, Hare, Garlington, & myself then mounted and proceeded to camp about six miles & a half. Soon after Dr. Harvey, Wetheral, and Thompson came in the ambulance, Weir and Eckerson tight, & Weir, he fell in the creek up to his neck. The guests came down to my tent and we finished a bottle of brandy Dr. Williams had given to me when I had a diarrhoea.

Got to bed by Eleven o'clock. Camped on Wolf Cr. Distance 20 1/2 miles.

Turtle Creek. *Sunday, 24th.* When we camped, we found driftwood for our fires and a mile further is another creek with wood and water. We crossed several small creeks and passed a number of old Lake beds, now dry, only two or three having any water & no wood. The country has very much the Topography of Minnesota and at no very distant day the lakes have had quite deep waters. We got to Turtle Creek at 3:30 plenty of water; & wood on the Mo. ½ mile— A ranch where mail stops. We got two chickens & some milk. Distance 27 ¾ miles.

This is where the diary ends. The regiment was back in Fort Lincoln, DT, at noon on 26 September, 1876.

List of supply items.

Canteens	5 .45 [*illegible*] 16	
N [nose] Bags	14+20+2	
" "	[?] 55	
C. [curry] Comb	[?] 35 ~~123~~ 39	74
" "	[?] 12+30	
H Brushes	[?] 23+16	39
" "	[?]...19+12+22	
Picket pins	[?]...26+1	27
Lariats	....25+4	29
?	15+25+2	
Surcingles	38+1	39
" "	3+11	
Saddle Blankets	24+3	27
" "	5+17+22+3+2	
Saddle Bags	15+1	17
" "	5+16+1	
Curb Bridles	3	
Cart[ridge] Boxes	25	
Pistol Holsters	5+1	
Carbines[?]	2	
Carbine Sling	+1+1	
" "	[?] 12+ 6	
Waist Belts	4+1+13	
" "	[?] 6+2	

Next page

Str?alts ath?n	28+1	
" "		
Cart[ridge Puch]	5+12	
" "	[?] 5	
Illegible	68	
Light[?] Knots	30	

Thongs	10 **10**	
" "	[?] *crossed out*	
Apron		
Cavalry[?] Complete	6	extra cartridges *faded* 3500 *illegible*
Waist belts		
" "		
" "		
Swivels	4+3	
" "	2	
Spurs	+1+10+9½	
" Shaps pr	1+2	
Canteens	33	
" "	40	
Slings	30+4	
Halters	20	
" Shaps	25	
Stirrups	22+20	

Next page—in addition to the items crossed out, the first eight lines have a large X drawn over them. Much of the bottom quarter of this page is obscured by dirty fingerprints.

~~Stirrups~~	~~[?] 4+4~~
Carbines	5 [*hash marks*]
Thong	1
H Brushes	12 [16] sm[?] 19 md[?]
C Combs	35 sm[?] 3 md[?]
Nose bags	14
Larriats	15 [msn?] 4 Sm[?]
~~Saddle Blankets~~	2
Haversacks	6
" ~~*illegible*~~	[msn?] 35
Stirrup	[msn?] 4+8
" [*illegible*] pr	4½ +65+16

Watering Bridles	[1-2] 15+1
Short girths	30+13
Curb bits & reins	10+35/31+4
Curb bits	[msn?] 22
Saddles	1+1
Curb[?] Stirrups	4+~~75~~ 62
" [msn?]	4
Halter *illegible*	16
Bridle H[ead] Stalls	35+10
Stirrup Straps	22 prs
~~illegible~~	
Halter straps	[?] 25+50
Cart[ridge] Pouches small[?]	25

Next page

Boots	13 in hashmarks
Shoes	1
Drawers	32 in hashmarks
Sh tents	13 in hashmarks
Sh[bbing] Brushes	33
Bedsacks	~~14 16~~ 20+16
" [msn?]	
Pillow case	1
Transport [msn?]	1 1 cot & table
Axe helves	5 [msn?]
Mosquito Bars	54
Forage Caps	69+73

Next page

Side Lines	1.+
" "	Mis[?] 24
Linens[?]	61
Carbines .50	1+2+4+1
Tables[?]	20+4+4-

Halter Chains	13
Pistol Cart[ridge] Pouches	8
" " "	14
" Cap Pouches	4
Clothing bags	3
Screw drivers	24
Tumbler pouches	19
String bi[?]s	3
Grain [?]ing	22
Firing pins	19

Next page

AUG MESS A/C

Aug 7 – Sept 6

Butter & Eggs	2.00
1 ½ tbs of Tea	1.00
[?] Hous &c	1.70
Potted Meats	1.50
5# cheese @ .50c [per] #	2.50
Crackers (?)	*Question mark in original, no price*
6# corned beef [?]	1.80
Yeast Powder	.50
6# Corn	1.25
Gibbs[1]	5.00
Chickens & Milk	1.25
Com[misary] Bill	17.85
Gibbs	5.00
This sum is off by five cents—	41.40
Sum is divided by two =	20.70
$11.20 is subtracted	11.20
The difference =	9.50
Addition	5.00

---

[1] This must be a loan to Pvt William Gibbs (1845–1934) the Company K butcher.

71

New sum =	14.50

Next page

MESS A/C

Aug 1 Hare cr	.70
Aug 7 Hare cr	2.00
~~Godfrey cr~~	~~2.50~~
Godfrey cr	1.00
	5.00
Sept 6 Hare cr	2.00
~~Potted Meats~~ H cr	1.50
Hare cr	2.50
" "	1.25
Godfrey cr	5.00
Hare cr	1.25
Hare cr Total	11.20

Last page

Mem[orandum]

Lt. Kell = four cap – 7 [cut off]

Trunk in hands of Burns with fine clothes. <u>Care.</u>

End [*written in original*]

Hare! Wants receipt for 4 "A" tents & poles, 6 camp kettles & 6 overalls

Mem: bridle & blanket

Miss: make up B. & send Harmon to give check or letter for more.

CUSTER'S LAST BATTLE.

BY ONE OF HIS TROOP COMMANDERS.

ON the 16th of April, 1876, at McComb City, Missouri, I received orders to report my troop ("K," 7th Cavalry) to the Commanding General of the Department of Dakota, at St. Paul, Minnesota. At the latter place about twenty-five recruits fresh from civil life joined the troop, and we were ordered to proceed to Fort Abraham Lincoln, Dakota, where the Yellowstone Expedition was being organized. This expedition consisted of the 7th United States Cavalry, commanded by General George A. Custer, 28 officers and about 700 men; two companies of the 17th United States Infantry, and one company of the 6th United States Infantry, 8 officers and 135 men; one platoon of Gatling guns, 2 officers and 32 men (of the 20th United States Infantry); and 40 "Ree" Indian scouts. The expeditionary forces were commanded by Brigadier-General Alfred H. Terry, the Department Commander, who with his staff arrived several days prior to our departure.

On the 17th day of May, at 5 a.m., the "general" [the signal to take down tents and break camp] was sounded, the wagons were packed and sent to the Quartermaster, and by six o'clock the wagon-train was on the road escorted by the infantry. By seven o'clock the 7th Cavalry was marching in column of platoon around the parade-ground of Fort Lincoln, headed by the band playing "Garry Owen," the Seventh's battle tune, first used when the regiment charged at the battle of Washita. The column was halted and dismounted just outside the garrison. The officers and married men were permitted to leave the ranks to say "good-by" to their families. General Terry, knowing the anxiety of the ladies, had assented to, or ordered, this demonstration, in order to allay their fears and satisfy them, by the formidable appearance we made, that we were able to cope with any enemy that we might expect to meet. Not many came out to witness the pageant, but many tear-filled eyes looked from the windows.

During this halt the wagon-train was assembled on the plateau west of the post and formed in column of fours. When it started off the "assembly" was sounded and absentees joined their commands. The signals "Mount" and "Forward" were sounded, and the regiment marched away, the band playing "The girl I left behind me."

The 7th Cavalry was divided into two columns, designated right and left wings, commanded by Major Marcus A. Reno and Captain F. W. Benteen. Each wing was subdivided into two battalions of three troops each. After the first day the following was the habitual order of march: one battalion was advance-guard, one was rear-guard, and one marched on each flank of the train. General Custer, with one troop of the advance-guard, went ahead and selected the route for the train and the camping-places at the end of the day's inarch. The other two troops of the advance-guard reported at headquarters for pioneer or fatigue duty, to build bridges and creek crossings. The rear-guard kept behind everything; when it came up to a wagon stalled in the mire, it helped to put the wagon forward. The battalions on the flanks were to keep within five hundred yards of the trail and not to get more than half a mile in advance or rear of the train. To avoid dismounting any oftener than necessary, the march was conducted as follows: one troop marched until about half a mile in advance of the train, when it was dismounted, the horses unbitted and allowed to graze until the train had passed and was about half a mile in advance of it, when it took up the march again; each of the other two troops would conduct their march in the same manner, so that two troops would be alongside the train all the time. If the country was much broken, a half dozen flankers were thrown out to guard against surprise. The flankers regulated their march so as to keep abreast of their troop. The pack-animals and beef herd were driven alongside the train by the packers and herders.

One wagon was assigned to each troop, and transported five days' rations and forage and the mess kit of the troop; also the mess kit, tents, and baggage of the troop officers and ten days' supplies for the officers' mess. The men were armed with the carbine and revolver; no one, not even the officer of the day, carried the saber. Each troop horse carried, in addition to the rider, between eighty and ninety pounds. This additional weight included all equipments and about one hundred rounds of ammunition. The wagon-train consisted in all of about one hundred and fifty wheeled vehicles. In it were carried thirty days' supplies of forage and rations (excepting beef), and two hundred rounds of ammunition per man. The two-horse wagons, hired by contract, carried from fifteen hundred to two thousand pounds. The six-mule government wagons carried from three to five thousand pounds, depending on the size and condition of the mules. The Gatling guns were each hauled by four condemned cavalry horses and marched in advance of the train. Two light wagons, loaded with axes, shovels, pickaxes and some pine boards and scantling, sufficient for a short bridge, accompanied the "pioneer" troops. The "crossings," as they are termed, were often very tedious and would frequently delay the train several hours. During this time the cavalry horses were unbitted and grazed, the men holding the reins. Those men not on duty at the crossing slept, or collected in groups to spin yarns and take a whiff at their "dingy dudeens." The officers usually collected near the crossing to watch progress, and passed the time in conversation and playing practical jokes. About noon the "strikers," who carried the haversacks, were called, and the different messes had their luncheon, sometimes separately, sometimes clubbing together. When the haversacks were opened, the horses usually stopped grazing and put their noses near their riders' faces and asked very plainly to share the hardtack; if their polite request did not receive attention they would paw the ground, or even strike their riders. The old soldier was generally willing to share with his beast.

The length of the day's march, varying from ten to forty miles, was determined in a great measure by the difficulties or obstacles encountered, by wood, water, and grass, and by the distance in advance where such advantages were likely to be found. If, about two or three o'clock in the afternoon, a column of smoke was seen in the direction of the trail and a mile or two in advance, it was a pretty sure indication that a camp had been selected. The cavalry, excepting the rear-guard, would then cut loose from the train and go directly to camp. The rear-guard would send details to collect fuel and unpack their wagons. The adjutant showed the wing commanders the general direction their lines of tents were to run, and the latter then directed the battalion or troop commanders to their camping-places. Generally one flank of each line would rest near the creek. The general form of the camp was that of a parallelogram. The wings camped on the long sides facing each other, and the headquarters and guard were located at one end nearest to the creek; the wagon-train was parked to close the other end and was guarded by the infantry battalion. The troops, as they arrived at their places, were formed in line, facing inward, dismounted, unsaddled, and, if the weather was hot and the sun shining, the men rubbed the horses' backs until dry. After this the horses were sent to water and put out to graze, with side-lines and lariats, under charge of the stable guard, consisting of one non-commissioned officer and three or six privates. The men of the troop then collected fuel, sometimes wood, often a mile or more distant from the camp; sometimes "buffalo chips." The main guard, consisting, usually, of four or five non-commissioned officers and twelve or fifteen privates, reported mounted at headquarters, and were directed to take posts on prominent points overlooking the camp and surrounding country, to guard against surprise. Each post consisted of one non-commissioned officer and three privates. The officer of the day, in addition to his ordinary duties in camp, had charge of the safety of the cavalry herds. Sometimes this latter duty was performed by an officer designated as "Officer of the Herd." To preserve the grazing in the immediate vicinity of the camp for evening and night grazing, all horses were required to be outside of the camp limits until retreat. When the train arrived, the headquarters and troop wagons went directly to the camping-place of their respective commands. The officers' baggage and tents were unloaded first; then the wagons went near the place where the troop kitchen was to be located, always on that flank of the troop farthest from headquarters. The teamsters unharnessed their mules and put them out to graze. The old stable guard reported to the troop commander for fatigue duty to put up the officers' tents and collect fuel for their mess. The troop officers' tents were usually placed twenty-five yards in rear of the line of men's tents and facing toward them. Their cook or mess tent was placed about ten or fifteen yards further to the rear. The "striker" made down the beds and arranged the "furniture," so to speak, which generally consisted of a camp-stool, tin washbasin, and a looking-glass. The men put up their tents soon after caring for their horses. The fronts of their tents were placed on a line established by stretching a picket-rope. The first sergeant's was on that flank of the line nearest to the headquarters. The horse equipments were placed on a line three yards in front of the tents. The men were not prohibited from using their saddles as pillows. A trench was dug for the mess fire, and the grass was burned around it for several yards to prevent prairie fires. After this the cooks busied themselves preparing supper. Beef was issued soon after the wagon-train came in, and the necessary number of beeves were butchered for the next day's issue; this was hauled in the wagons. Stable call was sounded about an hour before sunset The men of each troop were formed on the parade and marched to the horse herds by the first sergeant. Each man went to his own horse, took off the sidelines and fastened them around the horse's neck, then pulled the picket-pin, coiled the lariat, noosed the end fastened to the head halter around the horse's muzzle, mounted, and assembled in line at a place indicated by the first sergeant. The troop was then marched to the watering-place, which was usually selected with great care because of the boggy banks and miry, beds of the prairie streams. After watering, the horses were lariated outside but in the immediate vicinity of the camp. The ground directly in rear of the troop belonged to it, and was jealously guarded by those concerned against encroachment by others. After lariating their horses, the men got their currycombs, brushes, and nose-bags, and went to the troop wagon, where the quartermaster-sergeant and farrier measured, with tin cups, the forage to each man, each watching jealously that he got as much for his horse as those before him. He then went at once to feed and groom his horse. The officer whose duty it was to attend stables and the first sergeant superintended the grooming, examining each horse's back and feet carefully to see if they were all right. When a horse's back got sore through the carelessness of the rider, the man would generally be compelled to lead his horse until the sore was well. Immediately after stables, the cooks announced in a loud tone, "supper." The men with haversack and tin cup went to the mess fire and got their hardtack, meat, and coffee. If game had been killed the men did a little extra cooking themselves.

The troop officers' mess kits consisted of a sheet-iron cooking-stove, an iron kettle, stewing, frying, baking, and dish pans; a small Dutch oven, a camp-kettle, a mess-chest holding tableware for four persons, and a small folding-table. The table in fair weather was spread in the open air. The early part of the meal was a matter of business, but after the substantiate were stowed away, the delicacies were eaten more leisurely and time found for conversation. After supper the pipes were lighted, and the officers, if the weather was cold, went to the windward side of the campfire. Each man as he took his place was sure to poke or kick the fire, turn his back, hitch up his coat-tail, and fold his hands behind him.

Retreat was sounded a little after sunset and the roll was called, as much to insure the men having their equipments in place as to secure their presence, for it was not often we were near enough to any attraction to call the men away. (In 1876 there was not a ranch west of Bismarck, Dakota, nor east of Bozeman, Montana.) The stable guards began their tours of duty at this time. The non-commissioned officers reported to the troop commander for instructions for the night; these usually designated whether the horses were to be tied to the picket-line or kept out to graze, and included special instructions for the care of sick or weak horses. At dusk all horses were brought within the limits of the camp. The picket-line was stretched over three wagons in front of the men's tents, or three posts were used when remaining in camp over a day.

During the evening the men grouped about the fires and sang songs and spun yarns until "taps." The cooks prepared the breakfast, which usually consisted of hard bread, bacon, and coffee. If beans or fresh meat were to be cooked, the food was put into the Dutch ovens or camp-kettles, which were placed in the fire trench, covered over with hot ashes and coals, and a fire built over them. If the wind blew hard all fires were extinguished, to prevent prairie fires. The cooks were called an hour or an hour and a half before reveille. At the first call for reveille, usually 4.20 A.M., the stable guard wakened the occupants of each tent and the officer whose duty it was to attend the roll-call. Stable call followed reveille and was superintended by an officer. This occupied about three-quarters of an hour. Two hours after reveille, the command would be on the march. Of course there were incidents that occasionally relieved the monotony.

Antelope were very plentiful, and the men were encouraged by troop commanders to hunt. General Custer had a number of stag-hounds, which amused themselves and the command in their futile attempts to catch them. One morning they started up a large buck near where the column was marching; Lieutenant Hare immediately followed the hounds, passed them, drew his revolver, and shot the buck.

Nothing of special interest occurred until the 27th of May, when we came to the Bad Lands of the Little Missouri River. On the 30th General Custer was sent with four troops to make a scout up the Little Missouri, for about twenty miles. He returned the same day, without having discovered any recent "Indian signs." On the 31st we crossed the Little Missouri without difficulty. ON the 1st and 2d of June we were obliged to remain in camp on account of a snow-storm.

We remained in camp on the Powder River for three days. General Terry went to the Yellowstone [River] to communicate with the supply steamer *Far West*, which was at the mouth of the Powder River. He also went up the Yellowstone to communicate with General Gibbon's command, known as the "Montana Column," composed of four troops of the 2d Cavalry and several companies of the 7th Infantry. Before General Terry left it was given out that the 7th Cavalry would be sent to scout up the Powder River, while the wagon-train, escorted by the infantry, would be sent to establish a supply camp at the mouth of the Powder.

Eleven pack-mules, saddles, and aparejos were issued to each troop for this scout. This was a new departure; neither officers, men, nor mules had had any experience with this method of transportation. There were a few "packers" (civilian employes) to give instructions. Short, compactly built mules, the best for the purpose, were selected from the teams. A non-commissioned officer and four men of each troop were detailed for packers. After some instruction had been given by the professionals, especially how to tie the "diamond hitch," we concluded to make our maiden attempt by packing two empty water-casks. The mule was blinded and he submitted, with some uneasiness, to the packing. We supposed the packs were securely fastened and did not anticipate any trouble; but it is always the unexpected that happens with a mule. The blind was lifted; the mule gave a startled look first to one side, then to the other, at the two casks bandaged to his sides. He jumped to one side, causing to rattle a bung-plug that had fallen inside one of the casks. This startled him still more, and with head and tail high in the air he jumped again. He snorted and brayed, bucked and kicked, until the casks fell off. One was fastened to the saddle by the sling-rope. He now began to run, braying and making such a "rumpus" that the camp turned out as spectators. The affair excited serious concern lest all the animals in camp would be stampeded. When the cask was loose we got him back and made a second attempt with two sacks of grain. These he soon bucked off and then regaled himself with the spilt grain. As a final effort we concluded to try the aparejo, and pack two boxes of ammunition. This done, the mule walked off with as little concern as if he had been a pack-mule all his life.

General Terry having returned, orders were issued on the 10th for the right wing, six troops, under Major Reno, to make a scout up the Powder, provided with twelve days' rations.

The left wing was ordered to turn over all forage and rations; also the pack-mules, except four to each troop major Reno left at 3 p. M., and the next day the rest of the command marched to the mouth of the Powder. My troop was rear-guard, and at times we were over three miles in rear of the wagon-train waiting on the packers, for we had taken this opportunity to give them practical instruction.

Up to this time we had not seen an Indian, nor any recent signs of them, except one small trail of perhaps a half dozen tepees, evidently of a party of agency Indians on their way to join the hostile camps. The buffalo had all gone west; other game was scarce and wild. The indications were that the Indians were west of the Powder, and information from General Gibbon placed them south of the

Yellowstone. Some of the officers of the right wing before they left expressed their belief that we would not find any Indians, and were sanguine that we would rill get home by the middle of August.

Major Reno was ordered to scout to the forks of the Powder, then across to Mizpah Creek, follow it down to near its confluence with the Powder; then cross over to Pumpkin Creek, follow it down to the Tongue River, scout up that stream, and then rejoin the regiment at the mouth of the Tongue by the time his supplies were exhausted; unless, in the meantime, he should make some discovery that made it necessary to return sooner to make preparations for pursuit. A supply depot was established at the mouth of the Powder, guarded by the infantry, at which the wagon-train was left.

General Terry, with his staff and some supplies, took passage on the supply steamer *Far West,* and went up to the mouth of the Tongue. General Custer, with the left wing, marched to the mouth of the Tongue, where we remained until the 19th waiting tidings from Reno's scout. The grounds where we camped had been occupied by the Indians the previous winter. (Miles City, Montana, was first built on the site of this camp.) The rude shelters for their ponies, built of driftwood, were still standing and furnished fuel for our camp-fires. A number of their dead, placed upon scaffolds, or tied to the branches of trees, were disturbed and robbed of their trinkets. Several persons rode about exhibiting trinkets with as much gusto as if they were trophies of their valor, and showed no more concern for their desecration than if they had won them at a raffle. Ten days later I saw the bodies of these same persons dead, naked, and mutilated.

On the 19th of June tidings came from Reno that he had found a large trail that led up the Rosebud River. The particulars were not generally known. The camp was full of rumors; credulity was raised to the highest pitch, and we were filled with anxiety and curiosity until we reached Reno's command, and learned the details of their discoveries. They had found a large trail on the Tongue River, and had followed it up the Rosebud about forty miles. The number of lodges in the deserted villages was estimated by the number of camp-fires remaining to be about three hundred and fifty. The indications were that the trail was about three weeks old. No Indians had been seen, nor any recent signs. It is not probable that Reno's movements were known to the Indians, for on the very day Reno reached his farthest point up the Rosebud, the battle of the Rosebud, between General Crook's forces and the Indians, was fought. The two commands were then not more than forty miles apart, but neither knew nor even suspected the proximity of the other.

We reached the mouth of the Rosebud about noon on the 21st, and began preparations for the march and the battle of the Little Big Horn.

There were a number of Sioux Indians who never went to an agency except to visit friends and relatives. They camped in and roamed about the Buffalo Country. Their camp was the rendezvous for the agency Indians when they went out for their annual hunts for meat and robes. They were known as the "Hostiles," and comprised representatives from all the different tribes of the Sioux nation. Many of them were renegade outlaws from the agencies. In their visits to the agencies they were usually arrogant and fomenters of discord. Depredations had been made upon the commerce to the Black Hills, and a number of lives taken by them or by others, for which they were blamed. The authorities at Washington had determined to compel these Indians to reside at the agencies—hence the Sioux War. Sitting Bull, an Uncpapa Sioux Indian, was the chief of the hostile camp; he had about sixty lodges of followers on whom he could at all times depend. He was the host of the Hostiles, and as such received and entertained their visitors. These visitors gave him many presents, and he was thus enabled to make many presents in return. All visitors paid tribute to him, so he gave liberally to the most influential, the chiefs, i e., he "put it where it would do the most good." In this way he became known as the chief of the hostile Indian camp, and the camp was generally known as "Sitting Bull's camp." Sitting Bull was a heavy-set, muscular man, about five feet eight inches in stature, and at the time of the battle of the Little Big Horn was forty-two years of age. He was the autocrat of the camp— chiefly because he was the host. In council his views had great weight, because he was known as a great medicine man. He was a chief, but not a warrior chief. In the war councils he had a voice and vote the same as any other chief. A short time previous to the battle he had "made medicine," had predicted that the soldiers would attack them and that the soldiers would all be killed. He took no active part in the battle, but, as was his custom in time of danger, remained in the village "making medicine." Personally he was regarded as a great coward and a very great liar, "a man with a big head and a little heart." The command passed the remains of a "Sundance" lodge which took place about June 5, and to which I shall again refer. This was always a ceremony of great importance to the Indians. It ranks in interest and importance to the Indians with the graduation or commencement exercises of our civilized communities. In anticipation of this event, the Indians from the agencies had assembled at this camp.

Major James McLaughlin,[2] United States Indian Agent, stationed at the Devil's Lake Agency, Dakota, from 1870 to 1881, and at Standing Rock Agency, Dakota, from 1881 to the present time, has made it a point to get estimates of the number of Indians at the hostile camp at the time of the battle. In his opinion, and all who know him will accept it with confidence, about one-third of the whole Sioux nation, including the northern Cheyennes and Arapahoes, were present at the battle; he estimates the number present as between twelve and fifteen thousand; that one out of four is a low estimate in determining the number of warriors present; every male over fourteen years of age may be considered a warrior in a general fight such as was the battle of the Little Big Horn; also, considering the extra hazards of the hunt and expected battle, fewer squaws would accompany the recruits from the agencies. The minimum strength of their fighting men may then be put down as between twenty-five hundred and three thousand. Information was despatched from General Sheridan that from one agency alone about eighteen hundred lodges had set out to join the hostile camp; but that information did not reach General Terry until several days

---

[2] See McLaughlin's excellent memoir, *My Friend the Indian* (2014, BIG BYTE BOOKS).

after the battle. The principal warrior chiefs of the hostile Indians were: "Gall," "Crow King," and "Black Moon," Uncpapa Sioux; "Low Dog," "Crazy Horse," and "Big Road," Ogallala Sioux; "Spotted Eagle," Sans-Arc Sioux; "Hump" of the Minneconjous; and "White Bull" and "Little Horse," of the Cheyennes. To these belong the chief honors of conducting the battle, of whom, however, "Gall," "Crow King," and "Crazy Horse" were the ruling spirits.

Generals Terry, Gibbon, and Custer had a conference on board the steamer *Far West*. It was decided that the 7th Cavalry, under General Custer, should follow the trail discovered by Reno. "Officers' call" was sounded as soon as the conference had concluded. Upon assembling, General Custer gave us our orders. We were to transport on our pack-mules fifteen days' rations of hard bread, coffee, and sugar; twelve days' rations of bacon, and fifty rounds of carbine ammunition per man. Each man was to be supplied with 100 rounds of carbine and 24 rounds of pistol ammunition, to be carried on his person and in his saddle-bags. Each man was to carry on his horse twelve pounds of oats. The pack-mules sent out with Reno's command were badly used up, and promised seriously to embarrass the expedition. General Custer recommended that some extra forage be carried on the pack-mules. In endeavoring to carry out this recommendation some troop commanders foresaw the difficulties, and told the General that some of the mules would certainly break down, especially if the extra forage was packed. He replied in an excited manner, quite unusual with him: "Well, gentlemen, you may carry what supplies you please; you will be held responsible for your companies. The extra forage was only a suggestion, but this fact bear in mind, we will follow the trail for fifteen days unless we catch them before that time expires, no matter how far it may take us from our base of supplies; we may not see the supply steamer again;" and, turning as he was about to enter his tent, he added, "You had better carry along an extra supply of salt; we may have to live on horse meat before we get through." He was taken at his word, and an extra supply of salt was carried. "Battalion" and "tying" organizations were broken up, and troop commanders were responsible only to General Custer. His written instructions were as follows:

CAMP AT MOUTH OF ROSEBUD RIVER, MONTANA
TERRITORY, June 22d, 1876. LIEUTENANT-COLONEL CUSTER,
7TH CAVALRY.

COLONEL:

The Brigadier-General Commanding directs that, as soon as your regiment can be made ready for the march, you will proceed up the Rosebud in pursuit of the Indians whose trail was discovered by Major Reno a few days since. It is, of course, impossible to give you any definite instructions in regard to this movement, and were it not impossible to do so the Department Commander places too much confidence in your zeal, energy, and ability to wish to impose upon you precise orders which might hamper your action when nearly in contact with the enemy. He will, however, indicate to you his own views of what your action should be, and he desires that you should conform to them unless you shall see sufficient reason for departing from them. He thinks that you should proceed up the Rosebud until you ascertain definitely the direction in which the trail above spoken of leads. Should it be found (as it appears almost certain that it will be found) to turn towards the Little Horn, he thinks that you should still proceed southward, perhaps as far as the headwaters of the Tongue, and then turn towards the Little Horn, feeling constantly, however, to your left, so as to preclude the possibility of the escape of the Indians to the south or southeast by passing around your left flank. The column of Colonel Gibbon is now in motion for the mouth of the Big Horn. As soon as it reaches that point it will cross the Yellowstone and move up at least as far as the forks of the Big and Little Horns. Of course its future movements must be controlled by circumstances as they arise, but it is hoped that the Indians, if upon the Little Horn, may be so nearly inclosed by the two columns that their escape will be impossible.

The Department Commander desires that on your way up the Rosebud you should thoroughly examine the upper part of Tulloch's Creek, and that you should endeavor to send a scout through to Colonel Gibbon's column, with information of the result of your examination. The lower part of this creek will be examined *by a detachment from Colonel Gibbon's command. The supply steamer will be pushed up the Big Horn as far as the forks if the river is found to be navigable for that distance, and the Department Commander, who will accompany the column of Colonel Gibbon, desires you to report to him there not later than the expiration of the time for which your troops are rationed, unless in the meantime you receive further orders. Very respectfully, your obedient servant,*

E. W. SMITH, Captain 18th Infantry, Acting Assistant Adjutant-General.[3]

These instructions are explicit, and fixed the location of the Indians very accurately. Of course as soon as it was determined that we were to go out, nearly everyone took time to write letters home, but I doubt very much if there were many of a cheerful nature. Some officers made their wills; others gave verbal instructions as to the disposition of personal property and distribution of mementos; they seemed to have a presentiment of their fate.

At twelve o'clock, noon, on the 22d of June, the "Forward" was sounded, and the regiment marched out of camp in column of fours, each troop followed by its pack-mules. Generals Terry, Gibbon, and Custer stationed themselves near our line of march and reviewed the regiment. General Terry had a pleasant word for each officer as he returned the salute. Our pack-trains proved troublesome at the start, as the cargoes began falling off before we got out of camp, and during all that day the mules straggled badly. After that day, however, they were placed under the charge of an officer, who was directed to report at the end of each day's march the order of merit of the efficiency of the troop packers. Doubtless General Custer had some ulterior design in this. It is quite probable that if he had had occasion to detach troops requiring rapid marching, he would have selected those troops whose packers had the best records. At all events the efficiency was much increased, and after we struck the Indian trail the pack-trains kept well closed.

---

[3] Upon the interpretation of these orders rests nearly a century and a half of argument among military men, scholars, and students of the Little Bighorn battle. Did Custer disobey or exceed his orders?

We went into camp about 4 p.m., having marched twelve miles. About sunset "officers' call" was sounded, and we assembled at General Custer's bivouac and squatted in groups about the General's bed. It was not a cheerful assemblage; everybody seemed to be in a serious mood, and the little conversation carried on, before all had arrived, was in undertones. When all had assembled the General said that until further orders trumpet-calls would not be sounded except in an emergency; the marches would begin at 5 a.m. sharp; the troop commanders were all experienced officers, and knew well enough what to do, and when to do what was necessary for their troops; there were two things that would be regulated from his headquarters, i.e., when to move out of and when to go into camp. All other details, such as reveille, stables, watering, halting, grazing, etc., on the march would be left to the judgment and discretion of the troop commanders; they were to keep within supporting distance of each other, not to get ahead of the scouts, or very far to the rear of the column. He took particular pains to impress upon the officers his reliance upon their judgment, discretion, and loyalty. He thought, judging from the number of lodge fires reported by Reno, that we might meet at least a thousand warriors; there might be enough young men from the agencies, visiting their hostile friends, to make a total of fifteen hundred. He had consulted the reports of the Commissioner of Indian Affairs as to the probable number of "Hostiles" (those who had persistently refused to live or enroll themselves at the Indian agencies), and he was confident, if any reliance was to be placed upon those reports, that there would not be an opposing force of more than fifteen hundred. General Terry had offered him the additional force of the battalion of the 2d Cavalry, but he had declined it because he felt sure that the 7th Cavalry could whip any force that would be able to combine against him; that if the regiment could not, no other regiment in the service could; if they could whip the regiment, they would be able to defeat a much larger force, or, in other words, the reinforcement of this battalion, could not save us from defeat. With the regiment acting alone there would be harmony, but another organization would be sure to cause jealousy. He had declined the offer of the Gatling guns for the reason that they might hamper our movements or march at a critical moment, because of the difficult nature of the country through which we would march. The marches would be from twenty-five to thirty miles a day. Troop officers were cautioned to husband their rations and the strength of their mules and horses, as we might be out for a great deal longer time than that for which we were rationed, as he intended to follow the trail until we could get the Indians, even if it took us to the Indian agencies on the Missouri River or in Nebraska. All officers were requested to make to him, then or at any time, any suggestions they thought fit.

This "talk" of his, as we called it, was considered at the time as something extraordinary for General Custer, for it was not his habit to unbosom himself to his officers. In it he showed a lack of self-confidence, a reliance on somebody else; there was an indefinable something that was not Custer. His manner and tone, usually brusque and aggressive, or somewhat rasping, was on this occasion conciliating and subdued. There was something akin to an appeal, as if depressed, that made a deep impression on all present. We compared watches to get the official time, and separated to attend to our various duties. Lieutenants McIntosh, Wallace, and myself walked to our bivouac, for some distance in silence, when Wallace remarked: "Godfrey, I believe General Custer is going to be killed." "Why, Wallace," I replied, "what makes you think so?" "Because," said he, "I have never heard Custer talk in that way before."

I went to my troop and gave orders what time the "silent" reveille should be and as to other details for the morning preparations; also the following directions in case of a night attack: the stable guard, packers, and cooks were to go out at once to the horses and mules to quiet and guard them; the other men were to go at once to a designated rendezvous and await orders; no man should fire a shot until he received orders from an officer to do so. When they retired for the night they should put their arms and equipments where they could get them without leaving their beds. I then went through the herd to satisfy myself as to the security of the animals. During the performance of this duty I came to the bivouac of the Indian scouts. "Mitch" Bouyer, the half-breed interpreter, "Bloody Knife," the chief of the Ree scouts, "Half-Yellow-Face," the chief of the Crow scouts, and others were having a "talk." I observed them for a few minutes, when Bouyer turned toward me, apparently at the suggestion of "Half-Yellow-Face," and said, "Have you ever fought against these Sioux?" "Yes," I replied. Then he asked, "Well, how many do you expect to find?" I answered, "It is said we may find between one thousand and fifteen hundred." "Well, do you think we can whip that many?" "Oh, yes, I guess so." After he had interpreted our conversation, he said to me with a good deal of emphasis, "*Well, I can tell you we are going to have a big fight*"

At five o'clock, sharp, on the morning of the 23d, General Custer mounted and started up the Rosebud, followed by two sergeants, one carrying the regimental standard and the other his personal or headquarters flag, the same kind of flag as used while commanding his cavalry division during the Rebellion. This was the signal for the command to mount and take up the march. Eight miles out we came to the first of the Indian camping-places. It certainly indicated a large village and numerous population. There were a great many "wickiups" (bushes stuck in the ground with the tops drawn together, over which they placed canvas or blankets). These we supposed at the time were for the dogs, but subsequent events developed the fact that they were the temporary shelters of the transients from the agencies. During the day we passed through three of these camping-places and made halts at each one. Everybody was busy studying the age of pony droppings and tracks and lodge trails, and endeavoring to determine the number of lodges. These points were the all-absorbing topics of conversation. We went into camp about five o'clock, having marched about thirty-three miles.

June 24th we passed a great many camping places, all appearing to be of nearly the same strength. One would naturally suppose these were the successive camping-places of the same village, when in fact they were the continuous camps of the several bands. The fact that they appeared to be of nearly the same age, that is, having been made at the same time, did not impress us then. We passed through one much larger than any of the others. The grass for a considerable distance around it had been cropped close, indicating that large herds had been grazed there. The frame of a large "Sun-dance" lodge was standing, and in it we found the scalp of a white man, probably one of General Gibbon's command who had been killed some weeks previously. It was whilst here that the Indians from the agencies had joined the Hostiles' camp. The command halted here and "officers' call" was sounded. Upon assembling we were informed that our Crow scouts, who had been very active and efficient, had discovered fresh signs, the tracks of three or four ponies and of one Indian on foot. At this time a stiff southerly breeze was blowing; as we were about to separate, the General's headquarters flag was blown down, falling toward our rear. Being near the flag, I picked it up and stuck the staff in the ground, but it fell again to the rear. I then bored the staff into the ground where it would have the support of a sage-bush. This circumstance made no impression on me at the time, but after the battle an officer asked me if I remembered the incident; he had observed it, and regarded the fact of its falling to the rear as a bad omen, and felt sure we would suffer a defeat.

The march during the day was tedious. We made many long halts so as not to get ahead of the scouts, who seemed to be doing their work thoroughly, giving special attention to the right, toward Tulloch's Creek, the valley of which was in general view from the divide. Once or twice signal smokes were reported in that direction. The weather was dry and had been for some time, consequently the trail was very dusty. The troops were required to march on separate trails so that the dust clouds would not rise so high. The valley was heavily marked with lodge-pole trails and pony tracks, showing that immense herds of ponies had been driven over it About sundown we went into camp under the cover of a bluff, so as to hide the command as much as possible. We had marched about twenty-eight miles. The fires were ordered to be put out as soon as supper was over, and we were to be in readiness to march again at 11.30 p.m. Lieutenant Hare and myself lay down about 9.30 to take a nap; when comfortably fixed we heard someone say, "He's over there by that tree." As that described our locality pretty well, I called out to know what was wanted, and the reply came: "The General's compliments and wants to see all the officers at headquarters immediately." So we gave up our much-needed rest and groped our way through horse herds, oversleeping men, and through thickets of bushes trying to find headquarters. No one could tell us, and as all fires and lights were out we could not keep our bearings. We finally espied a solitary candle-light, toward which we traveled, and found most of the officers assembled at the General's bivouac. The General said that the trail led over the divide to the Little Big Horn; the march would be taken up at once, as he was anxious to get as near the divide as possible before daylight, where the command would be concealed during the day, and give ample time for the country to be studied, to locate the village and to make plans for the attack on the 26th. We then returned to our troops, except Lieutenant Hare, who was put on duty with the scouts.

Because of the dust it was impossible to see any distance, and the rattle of equipments and clattering of the horses' feet made it difficult to hear distinctly beyond our immediate surroundings. We could not see the trail, and we could only follow it by keeping in the dust cloud. The night was very calm, but occasionally a slight breeze would waft the cloud and disconcert our bearings; then we were obliged to halt to catch a sound from those in advance, sometimes whistling or hallooing, and getting a response we would start forward again. Finally troopers were put ahead, away from the noise of our column, and where they could hear the noise of those in front. A little after 2 a.m., June 25, the command was halted to await further tidings from the scouts; we had marched about ten miles. Part of the command unsaddled to rest the horses. After daylight some coffee was made, but it was almost impossible to drink it; the water was so alkaline that the horses refused to drink it. Sometime before eight o'clock, General Custer rode bareback to the several troops and gave orders to be ready to march at eight o'clock, and gave information that scouts had discovered the locality of the Indian villages or camps in the valley of the Little Big Horn, about twelve or fifteen miles beyond the divide. Just before setting out on the march I went to where General Custer's bivouac was. The General, "Bloody Knife," and several Ree scouts and a half-breed interpreter were squatted in a circle having a "talk," after the Indian fashion. The General wore a serious expression and was apparently abstracted. The scouts were doing the talking, and seemed nervous and disturbed. Finally "Bloody Knife" made a remark that recalled the General from his reverie, and he asked in his usual quick, brusque manner, "What's that he says?" The interpreter replied, "He says we'll find enough Sioux to keep us fighting two or three days." The General smiled and remarked, "I guess we'll get through with them in one day."

We started promptly at eight o'clock and marched uninterruptedly until 10.30 a.m., when we halted in a ravine and were ordered to preserve quiet, keep concealed, and not do anything that would be likely to reveal our presence to the enemy; we had marched about ten miles.

It is a rare occurrence in Indian warfare that gives a commander the opportunity to reconnoiter the enemy's position in daylight. This is particularly true if the Indians have a knowledge of the presence of troops in the country. When following an Indian trail the "signs" indicate the length of time elapsed since the presence of the Indians. When the "signs" indicate a "hot trail," i.e., near approach, the commander judges his distance and by a forced march, usually in the night-time, tries to reach the Indian village at night and make his disposition for a surprise attack at daylight. At all events his attack must be made with celerity, and generally without other knowledge of the numbers of the opposing force than that discovered or conjectured while following the trail. The dispositions for the attack may be said to be "made in the dark," and successful surprise to depend upon luck. If the advance to the attack be made in daylight it is next to impossible that a near approach can be made without discovery. In all our previous experiences, when the immediate presence of the troops was once known to them, the warriors swarmed to the attack, and resorted to all kinds of ruses to mislead the troops, to delay the advance toward their camp or village, while the squaws and children secured what personal effects they could, drove off the pony herd, and by flight put themselves beyond danger, and then scattering made successful pursuit next to impossible. In civilized warfare the hostile forces may confront each other for hours, days, or weeks, and the battle may be conducted with a tolerable knowledge of the numbers, position, etc., of each other. A full knowledge of the immediate presence of the enemy does not imply immediate attack. In Indian warfare the rule is "touch and go." These remarks are made because the firebrand nature of Indian warfare is not generally understood. In meditating upon the preliminaries of an Indian battle, old soldiers who have participated only in the battles of the Rebellion are apt to draw upon their own experiences for comparison, when there is no comparison.

The Little Big Horn River, or the "Greasy Grass" as it is known to the Indians, is a rapid mountain stream, from twenty to forty yards wide, with pebbled bottom, but abrupt, soft banks. The water at the ordinary stage is from two to five feet in depth, depending upon the width of the channel. The general direction of its course is northeasterly down to the Little Big Horn battlefield, where it trends northwesterly to its confluence with the Big Horn River. The other topographical features of the country which concern us in this narrative may be briefly described as follows: Between the Little Big Horn and Big Horn Rivers is a plateau of undulating prairie; between the Little Big Horn and the Rosebud are the Little Cherish or Wolf Mountains. By this it must not be misunderstood as a rocky upheaval chain or spur of mountains, but it is a rough, broken country of considerable elevation, of high precipitous hills and deep narrow gulches. The command had followed the trail up a branch of the Rosebud to within, say, a mile of the summit of these mountains, which form the "divide." Not many miles to our right was the divide between the Little Big Horn and Tulloch's Fork. The creek that drained the watershed to our right and front is now called "Sundance," or Benteen's, Creek. The trail, very tortuous, and sometimes dangerous, followed down the bed and valley of this creek, which at that time was dry for the greater part of its length. It was from the divide between the Little Big Horn and the Rosebud that the scouts had discovered the smoke rising above the village, and the pony herds grazing in the valley of the Little Big Horn, somewhere about twelve or fifteen miles away. It was to their point of view that General Custer had gone while the column was halted in the ravine. It was impossible for him to discover more of the enemy than had already been reported by the scouts. In consequence of the high bluffs which screened the village, it was not possible in following the trail to discover more. Nor was there a point of observation near the trail from which further discoveries could be made until the battle was at hand.

It was well known to the Indians that the troops were in the field, and a battle was fully expected by them; but the close proximity of our column was not known to them until the morning of the day of the battle. Several young men had left the hostile camp on that morning to go to one of the agencies in Nebraska. They saw the dust made by the column of troops; some of their number returned to the village and gave warning that the troops were coming, so the attack was not a surprise. For two or three days their camp had been pitched on the site where they were attacked. The place was not selected with the view to making that the battlefield of the campaign, but whoever was in the van on their march thought it a good place to camp, put up his tepee, and the others as they arrived followed his example. It is customary among the Indians to camp by bands. The bands usually camp some distance apart, and Indians of the number then together would occupy a territory of several miles along the river valley, and not necessarily within supporting distance of each other. But in view of the possible fulfilment of Sitting Bull's prophecy the village had massed.

Our officers had generally collected in groups and discussed the situation. Some sought solitude and sleep, or meditation. The Ree scouts, who had not been very active for the past day or two, were together and their "medicine man" was anointing them and invoking the Great Spirit to protect them from the Sioux. They seemed to have become satisfied that we were going to find more Sioux than we could well take care of.

Captain Yates's troop had lost one of its packs of hard bread during the night march from our last halting-place on the 24th. He had sent a detail back on the trail to recover it. Captain Keogh came to where a group of officers were, and said this detail had returned and reported that when near the pack they discovered an Indian opening one of the boxes of hard bread with his tomahawk, and that as soon as the Indian saw the soldiers he galloped away to the hills out of range and then moved along leisurely. This information was taken to the General at once by his brother, Colonel Tom Custer.

The General came back and had "officers' call" sounded. He recounted Captain Keogh's report, and also said that the scouts had seen several Indians moving along the ridge overlooking the valley through which we had marched, as if observing our movements; he thought the Indians must have seen the dust made by the command. At all events our presence had been discovered and further concealment was unnecessary; that we would march at once to attack the village; that he had not intended to make the attack until the next morning, the 26th, but our discovery made it imperative to act at once, as delay would allow the village to scatter and escape. Troop commanders were ordered to make a detail of one non-commissioned officer and six men to accompany the pack; to inspect their troops and report as soon as they were ready to march; that the troops would take their places in the column of march in the order in which reports of readiness were received, and that the last one to report would escort the pack-train.

The inspections were quickly made and the column was soon en route. We crossed the dividing ridge between the Rosebud and Little Big Horn valleys a little before noon. Shortly afterward the regiment was divided into battalions. The advance battalion, under Major Reno, consisted of troop "M," Captain French; troop "A," Captain Moylan and Lieutenant De Rudio; troop "G," Lieutenants McIntosh and Wallace; the Indian scouts under Lieutenants Varnum and Hare and the interpreter Girard; Lieutenant Hodgson was Acting Adjutant and Doctors De Wolf and Porter were the medical officers. The battalion under General Custer was composed of troop "I," Captain Keogh and Lieutenant Porter; troop "F," Captain Yates and Lieutenant Reily; troop "C," Captain Custer and Lieutenant Harrington; troop "E," Lieutenants Smith and Sturgis; troop "L," Lieutenants Calhoun and Crittenden; Lieutenant Cook was the Adjutant, and Dr. G. E. Lord was medical officer. The Battalion under Captain Benteen consisted of troop "H," Captain Benteen and Lieutenant Gibson; troop "D," Captain Weir and Lieutenant Edgerly, and troop "K," Lieutenant Godfrey. The pack-train, Lieutenant

Mathey in charge, was under the escort of troop "B," Captain McDougall.

Major Reno's battalion marched down a valley that developed into the small tributary to the Little Big Horn, now called "Sundance," or Benteen's, Creek. The Indian trail followed the meanderings of this valley. Custer's column followed Reno's closely, and the pack-train followed their trail. Benteen's battalion was ordered to the left and front, to a line of high bluffs about three or four miles distant. Benteen was ordered if he saw anything to send word to Custer, but to pitch into anything he came across; if, when he arrived at the high bluffs, he could not see any enemy, he should continue his march to the next line of bluffs and so on, until he could see the Little Big Horn Valley. He marched over a succession of rough, steep hills and deep valleys. The view from the point where the regiment was organized into battalions did not discover the difficult nature of the country, but as we advanced farther it became more and more difficult and more forbidding. Lieutenant Gibson was sent some distance in advance but saw no enemy, and so signaled the result of his reconnaissance to Benteen. The obstacles threw the battalion by degrees to the right until we came in sight of and not more than a mile from the trail. Many of our horses were greatly jaded by the climbing and descending, some getting far to the rear of the column. Benteen very wisely determined to follow the trail of the rest of the command, and we got into it just in advance of the pack-train. During this march on the left we could see occasionally the battalion under Custer, distinguished by the troop mounted on gray horses, marching at a rapid gait. Two or three times we heard loud cheering and also some few shots, but the occasion of these demonstrations is not known.

Sometime after getting on the trail we came to a water-hole, or morass, at which a stream of running water had its source. Benteen halted the battalion. While watering we heard some firing in advance, and Weir became a little impatient at the delay of watering and started off with his troop, taking the advance, whereas his place in column was second. The rest of the battalion moved out very soon afterward and soon caught up with him. Just as we were leaving the water-hole the pack-train was arriving, and the poor thirsty mules plunged into the morass in spite of the efforts of the packers to prevent them, for they had not had water since the previous evening. We passed a burning tepee, fired presumably by our scouts, in which was the body of a warrior who had been killed in the battle with Crook's troops on the Rosebud on the 17th of June.

The battalions under Reno and Custer did not meet any Indians until Reno arrived at the burning tepee; here a few were seen. These Indians did not act as if surprised by the appearance of troops; they made no effort to delay the column, but simply kept far enough in advance to invite pursuit. Reno's command and the scouts followed them closely, until he received orders "to move forward at as rapid a gait as he thought prudent, and charge the village afterward, and the whole outfit would support him." The order was received when Reno was not very far from the Little Big Horn River. His battalion moved at a trot to the river, where Reno delayed about ten or fifteen minutes watering the horses and reforming the column on the left bank of the stream. Reno now sent word to Custer that he had everything in front of him and that the enemy was strong. Custer had moved off to the right, being separated from Reno by a line of high bluffs and the river. Reno moved forward in column of fours about half a mile, then formed the battalion in line of battle across the valley with the scouts on the left; after advancing about a mile further he deployed the battalion as [dismounted] skirmishers. In the meantime the Hostiles, continually reinforced, fell back, firing occasionally, but made no decided effort to check Reno's advance. The horses of two men became unmanageable and carried them into the Indian camp. The Indians now developed great force, opened a brisk fire, mounted, and made a dash toward the foothills on the left flank where the Ree scouts were. The scouts ignominiously fled, most of them abandoning the field altogether.

Reno, not seeing the "whole outfit" within supporting distance, did not obey his orders to charge the village, but dismounted his command to fight on foot. The movements of the Indians around the left flank and the flight of the scouts caused the left to fall back until the command was on the defensive in the timber and covered by the bank of the old riverbed. Reno's loss thus far was one wounded. The position was a strong one, well protected in front by the bank and fringe of timber, somewhat open in the rear, but sheltered by timber in the bottom. Those present differ in their estimates of the length of time the command remained in the bottom after they were attacked in force. Some say "a few minutes"; others, "about an hour." While Reno remained there his casualties were few. The Hostiles had him nearly surrounded, and there was some firing from the rear of the position by Indians on the opposite bank of the river. One man [Bloody Knife] was killed close to where Reno was, and directly afterward Reno gave orders to those near him to "mount and get to the bluffs." This order was not generally heard or communicated; while those who did hear it were preparing to execute it, he countermanded the order, but soon afterward he repeated the same order, "to mount and get to the bluffs," and again it was not generally understood. Individuals, observing the preparations of those on the left, near Reno, informed their troop commanders, who then gave orders to mount. Owing to the noise of the firing and to the absorbed attention they were giving to the enemy, many did not know of the order until too late to accompany the command. Some remained concealed until the Indians left and then came out. Four others remained until night and then escaped. Reno's command left the bottom by troop organizations in column. Reno was with the foremost in this retreat or "charge," as he termed it in his report, and after he had exhausted the shots of his revolvers he threw them away. The hostile strength pushed Reno's retreat to the left, so he could not get to the ford where he had entered the valley, but they were fortunate in striking the river at a fordable place; a pony-trail led up a funnel shaped ravine into the bluffs. Here the command got jammed and lost all semblance of organization. The Indians fired into them, but not very effectively. There does not appear to have been any resistance, certainly no organized resistance, during this retreat. On the right and left of the ravine into which the pony-path led were rough precipitous clay bluffs. It was surprising to see what steep inclines men and horses clambered up under the excitement of danger.

98

Lieutenant Donald McIntosh was killed soon after leaving the timber. Dr. De Wolf was killed while climbing one of the bluffs a short distance from the command. Lieutenant B. H. Hodgson's horse leaped from the bank into the river and fell dead; the lieutenant was wounded in the leg, probably by the same bullet that killed the horse. Hodgson called out, "For God's sake, don't abandon me;" he was assured that he would not be left behind. Hodgson then took hold of a comrade's stirrup strap and was taken across the stream, but soon after was shot and killed. Hodgson, some days before the battle, had said that if he was dismounted in battle or wounded, he intended to take hold of somebody's stirrup to assist himself from the field. During the retreat Private Dalvern, troop "F," had a hand-to-hand conflict with an Indian; his horse was killed; he then shot the Indian, caught the Indian's pony, and rode to the command.

Reno's casualties thus far were three officers, including Dr. J. M. De Wolf,[4] and twenty-nine enlisted men and scouts killed; seven enlisted men wounded; and one officer, one interpreter, and fourteen soldiers and scouts missing. Nearly all the casualties occurred during the retreat and after leaving the timber. The Ree scouts continued their flight until they reached the supply camp at the mouth of the Powder, on the 27th. The Crow scouts remained with the command.

We will now go back to Benteen's battalion. Not long after leaving the water-hole a sergeant met him with an order from Custer to the commanding officer of the pack-train to hurry it up. The sergeant was sent back to the train with the message; as he passed the column he said to the men, "We've got'em, boys." From this and other remarks we inferred that Custer had attacked and captured the village.

Shortly afterward we were met by a trumpeter bearing this message signed by Colonel Cook, Adjutant: *"Benteen, come on. Big*

---

[4] James Madison DeWolf (1843–June 25, 1876) served in the Civil War and was wounded, returning to active duty. After the war, he graduated in medicine from Harvard University and in 1875 signed a contract with the US Army as an Acting Assistant Surgeon.

village. Be quick. Bring packs," with the postscript, *"Bring packs."* The column had been marching at a trot and walk, according as the ground was smooth or broken. We now heard firing, first straggling shots, and as we advanced the engagement became more and more pronounced and appeared to be coming toward us. The column took the gallop with pistols drawn, expecting to meet the enemy which we thought Custer was driving before him in his effort to communicate with the pack-train, never suspecting that our force had been defeated. We were forming in line to meet our supposed enemy, when we came in full view of the valley of the Little Big Horn. The valley was full of horsemen riding to and fro in clouds of dust and smoke, for the grass had been fired by the Indians to drive the troops out and cover their own movements. On the bluffs to our right we saw a body of troops and that they were engaged. But an engagement appeared to be going on in the valley too. Owing to the distance, smoke, and dust, it was impossible to distinguish if those in the valley were friends or foes. There was a short time of uncertainty as to the direction in which we should go, but some Crow scouts came by, driving a small herd of ponies, one of whom said "Soldiers," and motioned for the command to go to the right. Following his directions, we soon joined Reno's battalion, which was still firing. Reno had lost his hat and had a handkerchief tied about his head, and appeared to be very much excited.

Benteen's battalion was ordered to dismount and deploy as skirmishers on the edge of the bluffs overlooking the valley. Very soon after this the Indians withdrew from the attack. Lieutenant Hare came to where I was standing and, grasping my hand heartily, said with a good deal of emphasis: "We've had a big fight in the bottom, got whipped, and I am glad to see you." I was satisfied that he meant what he said, for I had already suspected that something was wrong, but was not quite prepared for such startling information. Benteen's battalion was ordered to divide its ammunition with Reno's men, who had apparently expended nearly all in their personal possession. It has often been a matter of doubt whether this was a fact, or the effect of imagination. It seems most improbable, in view of their active movements and the short time the command was firing, that the "most of the men" should have expended one hundred and fifty rounds of ammunition per man.

While waiting for the ammunition pack-mules, Major Reno concluded to make an effort to recover and bury the body of Lieutenant Hodgson. At the same time we loaded up a few men with canteens to get water for the command; they were to accompany the rescuing party. The effort was futile; the party was ordered back after being fired upon by some Indians who doubtless were scalping the dead near the foot of the bluffs.

A number of officers collected on the edge of the bluff overlooking the valley and were discussing the situation; among our number was Captain Moylan, a veteran soldier, and a good one too, watching intently the scene below. Moylan remarked, quite emphatically: "Gentlemen, in my opinion General Custer has made the biggest mistake of his life, by not taking the whole regiment in at once in the first attack." At this time there were a large number of horsemen, Indians, in the valley. Suddenly they all started down the valley, and in a few minutes scarcely a horseman was to be seen. Heavy firing was heard down the river. During this time the questions were being asked: "What's the matter with Custer, that he don't send word what we shall do?" "Wonder what we are staying here for?" etc., thus showing some uneasiness; but still no one seemed to show great anxiety, nor do I know that anyone felt any serious apprehension but that Custer could and would take care of himself. Some of Reno's men had seen a party of Custer's command, including Custer himself, on the bluffs about the time the Indians began to develop in Reno's front. This party was heard to cheer, and seen to wave their hats as if to give encouragement, and then they disappeared behind the hills or escaped further attention from those below. It was about the time of this incident that Trumpeter Martini left Cook with Custer's last orders to Benteen, viz.: *"Benteen, come on. Big village. Be quick. Bring packs. Cook, Adjutant. P. S. Bring packs."* The repetition in the order would seem to indicate that Cook was excited, flurried, or that he wanted to emphasize the necessity for escorting the packs. It is possible, yes probable, that from the high point Custer could then see nearly the whole camp and force of the

Indians and realized that the chances were desperate; but it was too late to reunite his forces for the attack. Reno was already in the fight and his (Custer's) own battalion was separated from the attack by a distance of two and a half to three miles. He had no reason to think that Reno would not push his attack vigorously. A commander seldom goes into battle counting upon the failure of his lieutenant; if he did, he certainly would provide that such failure should not turn into disaster.

During a long time after the junction of Reno and Benteen we heard firing down the river in the direction of Custer's command. We were satisfied that Custer was fighting the Indians somewhere, and the conviction was expressed that "our command ought to be doing something or Custer would be after Reno with a sharp stick." We heard two distinct volleys which excited some surprise, and, if I mistake not, brought out the remark from someone that "Custer was giving it to them for all he was worth." I have but little doubt now that these volleys were fired by Custer's orders as signals of distress and to indicate where he was.

Captain Weir and Lieutenant Edgerly, after driving the Indians away from Reno's command, on their side, heard the firing, became impatient at the delay, and thought they would move down that way, if they should be permitted. Weir started to get this permission, but changed his mind and concluded to take a survey from the high bluffs first. Edgerly, seeing Weir going in the direction of the firing, supposed it was all right and started down the ravine with the troop. Weir, from the high point, saw the Indians in large numbers start for Edgerly, and signaled for him to change his direction, and Edgerly went over to the high point, where they remained, not seriously molested, until the remainder of the troops marched down there; the Indians were seen by them to ride about what afterward proved to be Custer's battlefield, shooting into the bodies of the dead men.

McDougall came up with the pack-train and reported the firing when he reported his arrival to Reno. I remember distinctly looking at my watch at twenty minutes past four, and made a note of it in my memorandum-book, and although I have never satisfactorily been able to recall what particular incident happened at that time, it was some important event before we started down the river. It is my impression, however, that it was the arrival of the pack-train. It was about this time that thirteen men and a scout named Herendeen[5] rejoined the command; they had been missing since Reno's flight from the bottom; several of them were wounded. These men had lost their horses in the stampede from the bottom and had remained in the timber; when leaving the timber to rejoin, they were fired upon by five Indians, but they drove them away and were not again molested.

My recollection is that it was about half-past two when we joined Reno. About five o'clock the command moved down toward Custer's supposed whereabouts, intending to join him. The advance went as far as the high bluffs where the command was halted. Persons who have been on the plains and have seen stationary objects dancing before them, now in view and now obscured, or a weed on the top of a hill, projected against the sky, magnified to appear as a tree, will readily understand why our views would be unsatisfactory. We could see stationary groups of horsemen, and individual horsemen moving about; from their grouping and the manner in which they sat their horses we knew they were Indians. On the left of the valley a strange sight attracted our attention. Someone remarked that there had been a fire that scorched the leaves of the bushes, which caused the reddish-brown appearance, but this appearance was changeable; watching this intently for a short time with field-glasses, it was discovered that this strange sight was the immense pony-herds of the Indians.

Looking toward Custer's field, on a hill two miles away we saw a large assemblage. At first our command did not appear to attract their attention, although there was some commotion observable among those nearer to our position. We heard occasional shots, most of which seemed to be a great distance off, beyond the large groups on the hill. While watching this group the conclusion was

---

[5] George B. Herendeen (1848–1919) was a pioneer of Bozeman, Montana Territory, cowboy, prospector, explorer, scout, and saloon keeper (oclc.org; ArchiveGrid, 2021). He testified at the 1879 Reno Court of Inquiry.

arrived at that Custer had been repulsed, and the firing was the parting shots of the rear-guard. The firing ceased, the groups dispersed, clouds of dust arose from all parts of the field, and the horsemen converged toward our position. The command was now dismounted to fight on foot. Weir's and French's troops were posted on the high bluffs and to the front of them; my own troop along the crest of the bluffs next to the river; the rest of the command moved to the rear, as I supposed to occupy other points in the vicinity, to make this our defensive position. Busying myself with posting my men, giving direction about the use of ammunition, etc., I was a little startled by the remark that the command was out of sight. At this time Weir's and French's troops were being attacked. Orders were soon brought to me by Lieutenant Hare, Acting-Adjutant, to join the main command. I had gone some distance in the execution of this order when, looking back, I saw French's troop come tearing over the bluffs, and soon after Weir's troop followed in hot haste. Edgerly was near the top of the bluff trying to mount his frantic horse, and it did seem that he would not succeed, but he vaulted into his saddle and then joined the troop. The Indians almost immediately followed to the top of the bluff, and commenced firing into the retreating troops, killing one man, wounding others and several horses. They then started down the hillside in pursuit. I at once made up my mind that such a retreat and close pursuit would throw the whole command into confusion, and, perhaps, prove disastrous. I dismounted my men to fight on foot, deploying as rapidly as possible without waiting for the formation laid down in tactics. Lieutenant Hare expressed his intention of staying with me, "Adjutant or no Adjutant." The led horses were sent to the main command. Our fire in a short time compelled the Indians to halt and take cover, but before this was accomplished, a second order came for me to fall back as quickly as possible to the main command. Having checked the pursuit we began our retreat, slowly at first, but kept up our firing. After proceeding some distance the men began to group together, and to move a little faster and faster, and our fire slackened. This was pretty good evidence that they were getting demoralized. The Indians were being heavily reinforced, and began to come from their cover, but kept up a heavy fire. I halted the line, made the men take their intervals, and again drove the Indians to cover; then once more began the retreat. The firing of the Indians was very heavy; the bullets struck the ground all about us; but the "ping-ping" of the bullets overhead seemed to have a more terrifying influence than the "swish-thud" of the bullets that struck the ground immediately about us. When we got to the ridge in front of Reno's position I observed some Indians making all haste to get possession of a hill to the right. I could now see the rest of the command, and I knew that that hill would command Reno's position. Supposing that my troop was to occupy the line we were then on, I ordered Hare to take ten men and hold the hill, but, just as he was moving off, an order came from Reno to get back as quickly as possible; so I recalled Hare and ordered the men to run to the lines. This movement was executed, strange to say, without a single casualty.

The Indians now took possession of all the surrounding high points, and opened a heavy fire. They had in the meantime sent a large force up the valley, and soon our position was entirely surrounded. It was now about seven o'clock.

Our position next the river was protected by the rough, rugged steep bluffs which were cut up by irregular deep ravines. From the crest of these bluffs the ground gently declined away from the river. On the north there was a short ridge, the ground sloping gently to the front and rear. This ridge, during the first day, was occupied by five troops. Directly in rear of the ridge was a small hill; in the ravine on the south of this hill our hospital was established, and the horses and pack-mules were secured. Across this ravine one troop, Moylan's, was posted, the packs and dead animals being utilized for breastworks. The high hill on the south was occupied by Benteen's troop. Everybody now lay down and spread himself out as thin as possible. After lying there a few minutes I was horrified to find myself wondering if a small sage-bush, about as thick as my finger, would turn a bullet, so I got up and walked along the line, cautioned the men not to waste their ammunition; ordered certain men who were good shots to do the firing, and others to keep them supplied with loaded guns.

The firing continued till nearly dark (between nine and ten o'clock), although after dusk but little attention was paid to the firing, as everybody moved about freely.

Of course everybody was wondering about Custer—why he did not communicate by courier or signal. But the general opinion seemed to prevail that he had been defeated and driven down the river, where he would probably join General Terry, and with whom he would return to our relief. Quite frequently, too, the question, "What's the matter with Custer?" would evoke an impatient reply.

Indians are proverbial economists of fuel, but they did not stint themselves that night. The long twilight was prolonged by numerous bonfires, located throughout their village. The long shadows of the hills and the refracted light gave a supernatural aspect to the surrounding country, which may account for the illusions of those who imagined they could see columns of troops, etc. Although our dusky foes did not molest us with obtrusive attentions during the night, yet it must not be inferred that we were allowed to pass the night in perfect rest; or that they were endeavoring to soothe us into forgetfulness of their proximity, or trying to conceal their situation. They were a good deal happier than we were; nor did they strive to conceal their joy. Their camp was a veritable pandemonium. All night long they continued their frantic revels; beating tom-toms, dancing, whooping, yelling with demoniacal screams, and discharging firearms. We knew they were having a scalp-dance. In this connection the question has often been asked "if they did not have prisoners at the torture?" The Indians deny that they took any prisoners. We did not discover any evidence of torture in their camps. It is true that we did find human heads severed from their bodies, but these probably had been paraded in their orgies during that terrible night.

Our casualties had been comparatively few since taking position on the hill. The question of moving was discussed, but the conditions coupled to the proposition caused it to be indignantly rejected.[6] Some of the scouts were sent out soon after dark to look

---

[6] Godfrey is probably referring to Reno's suggestion to Benteen of a retreat

for signs of Custer's command, but they returned after a short absence saying that the country was full of Sioux. Lieutenant Varnum volunteered to go out, but was either discouraged from the venture or forbidden to go out.

After dark the troops were arranged a little differently. The horses were unsaddled, and the mules were relieved of their packs; all animals were secured to lariats stretched and picketed to the ground.

Soon after all firing had ceased the wildest confusion prevailed. Men imagined they could see a column of troops over on the hills or ridges, that they could hear the tramp of the horses, the command of officers, or even the trumpet-calls. Stable-call was sounded by one of our trumpeters; shots were fired by some of our men, and familiar trumpet-calls were sounded by our trumpeter immediately after, to let the supposed marching column know that we were friends. Every favorable expression or opinion was received with credulity, and then ratified with a cheer. Somebody suggested that General Crook might be coming, so someone, a civilian packer, I think, mounted a horse, and galloping along the line yelled: "Don't be discouraged, boys, Crook is coming." But they gradually realized that the much-wished-for reinforcements were but the phantasma of their imaginations, and settled down to their work of digging rifle-pits. They worked in pairs, in threes and fours. The ground was hard and dry. There were only three or four spades and shovels in the whole command; axes, hatchets, knives, table-forks, tin cups, and halves of canteens were brought into use. However, everybody worked hard, and some were still digging when the enemy opened fire at early dawn, between half-past two and three o'clock, so that all had some sort of shelter, except Benteen's men. The enemy's first salutations were rather feeble, and our side made scarcely any response; but as dawn advanced to daylight their lines were heavily reinforced, and both sides kept up a continuous fusillade. Of course it was their policy to draw our fire as much as possible to exhaust our ammunition. As they exposed their persons very little we forbade

---

that would leave wounded on the field. Godfrey did not hear about this until many years after the battle, when he had to drag it out of Benteen.

our men, except well-known good shots, to fire without orders. The Indians amused themselves by standing erect, in full view for an instant, and then dropping down again before a bullet could reach them, but of that they soon seemed to grow tired or found it too dangerous; then they resorted to the old ruse of raising a hat and blouse, or a blanket, on a stick to draw our fire; we soon understood their tactics. Occasionally they fired volleys at command. Their fire, however, was not very effective. Benteen's troop suffered greater losses than any other, because their rear was exposed to the long-range firing from the hills on the north. The horses and mules suffered greatly, as they were fully exposed to long-range fire from the east.

Benteen came over to where Reno was lying, and asked for reinforcements to be sent to his line. Before he left his line, however, he ordered Gibson not to fall back under any circumstances, as this was the key of the position. Gibson's men had expended nearly all their ammunition, some men being reduced to as few as four or five cartridges. He was embarrassed, too, with quite a number of wounded men. Indeed, the situation here was most critical, for if the Indians had made a rush, a retreat was inevitable. Private McDermott volunteered to carry a message from Gibson to Benteen urging him to hasten the reinforcements. After considerable urging by Benteen, Reno finally ordered French to take "M" troop over to the south side. On his way over Benteen picked up some men then with the horses. Just previous to his arrival an Indian had shot one of Gibson's men, then rushed up and touched the body with his "coup-stick," and started back to cover, but he was killed. He was in such close proximity to the lines and so exposed to the fire that the other Indians could not carry his body away. This, I believe, was the only dead Indian left in our possession. This boldness determined Benteen to make a charge, and the Indians were driven nearly to the river. On their retreat they dragged several dead and wounded warriors away with them.

The firing almost ceased for a while, and then it recommenced with greater fury. From this fact, and their more active movements, it became evident that they contemplated something more serious than a mere fusillade. Benteen came back to where Reno was, and said if something was not done pretty soon the Indians would run into our lines. Waiting a short time, and no action being taken on his suggestion, he said rather impatiently: "You've got to do something here pretty quick; this won't do, you must drive them back." Reno then directed us to get ready for a charge, and told Benteen to give the word. Benteen called out "All ready now, men. Now's your time. Give them hell. Hip, hip, here we go!" and away we went with a hurrah, every man, but one who lay in his pit crying like a child. The Indians fired more rapidly than before from their whole line. Our men left the pits with their carbines loaded, and they began firing without orders soon after we started. A large body of Indians had assembled at the foot of one of the hills, intending probably to make a charge, as Benteen had divined, but they broke as soon as our line started. When we had advanced 75 or 100 yards, Reno called out "Get back, men, get back," and back the whole line came. A most singular fact of this sortie was that not a man who advanced with the lines was hit; but directly after everyone had gotten into the pits again, the one man who did not go out was shot in the head and killed instantly. The poor fellow had a premonition that he would be killed, and had so told one of his comrades.

Up to this time the command had been without water. The excitement and heat made our thirst almost maddening. The men were forbidden to use tobacco. They put pebbles in their mouths to excite the glands; some ate grass roots, but did not find relief; some tried to eat hard bread, but after chewing it awhile would blow it out of their mouths like so much flour. A few potatoes were given out and afforded some relief. About 11 a.m. the firing was slack, and parties of volunteers were formed to get water under the protection of Benteen's lines. The parties worked their way down the ravines to within a few yards of the river. The men would get ready, make a rush to the river, fill the camp-kettles, and return to fill the canteens. Some Indians stationed in a copse of woods, a short distance away, opened fire whenever a man exposed himself, which made this a particularly hazardous service. Several men were wounded, and the additional danger was then incurred of rescuing their wounded comrades. I think all these men were rewarded with Medals of

Honor. By about one o'clock the Indians had nearly all left us, but they still guarded the river; by that time, however, we had about all the water we needed for immediate use. About two o'clock the Indians came back, opened fire, and drove us to the trenches again, but by three o'clock the firing had ceased altogether.

Late in the afternoon we saw a few horsemen in the bottom apparently to observe us, and then fire was set to the grass in the valley. About 7 p.m. we saw emerge from behind this screen of smoke an immense moving mass crossing the plateau, going toward the Big Horn Mountains. A fervent "Thank God" that they had at last given up the contest was soon followed by grave doubts as to their motive for moving. Perhaps Custer had met Terry, and was coming to our relief. Perhaps they were short of ammunition, and were moving their village to a safe distance before making a final desperate effort to overwhelm us. Perhaps it was only a ruse to get us on the move, and then clean us out.

The stench from the dead men and horses was now exceedingly offensive, and it was decided to take up a new position nearer the river. The companies were assigned positions, and the men were put to work digging pits with the expectation of a renewal of the attack. Our loss on the hill had been eighteen killed and fifty-two wounded.

During the night Lieutenant DeRudio, Private O'Neal, Mr. Girard, the interpreter, and Jackson, a half-breed scout, came to our line. They had been left in the bottom when Reno made his retreat.

In this narrative of the movements immediately preceding, and resulting in, the annihilation of the men with Custer, I have related facts substantially as observed by myself or as given to me by Chief Gall of the Sioux. His statements have been corroborated by other Indians, notably the wife of "Spotted Horn Bull," an intelligent Sioux squaw, one of the first who had the courage to talk freely to anyone who participated in the battle.

In 1886, on the tenth anniversary, an effort was made to have a reunion of the survivors at the battlefield. Colonel Benteen, Captains McDougall and Edgerly, Dr. Porter, Sergeant Hall, Trumpeter Penwell, and myself met there on the 25th of June. Through the kind efforts of the officers and of the ladies at Fort Custer our visit was made as pleasant as possible. Through the personal influence of Major McLaughlin, Indian agent at Standing Rock Agency, Chief Gall was prevailed upon to accompany the party and describe Custer's part in the battle. We were unfortunate in not having an efficient and truthful interpreter on the field at the reunion. The statements I have used were, after our return to the agency, interpreted by Mrs. McLaughlin and Mr. Farribault,[7] of the agency, both of whom are perfectly trustworthy and are familiar with the Sioux language.

It has been previously noted that General Custer separated from Reno before the latter crossed the Little Big Horn under orders to charge the village. Custer's column bore to the right of the river (a sudden change of plan, probably); a ridge of high bluffs and the river separated the two commands, and they could not see each other. On this ridge, however, Custer and staff were seen to wave their hats, and heard to cheer just as Reno was beginning the attack; but Custer's troops were at that time a mile or more to his right. It was about this time that the trumpeter was sent back with Custer's last order to Benteen. From this place Custer could survey the valley for several miles above and for a short distance below Reno; yet he could only see a part of the village; he must, then, have felt confident that all the Indians were below him: hence, I presume, his message to Benteen. The view of the main body of the village was cut off by the highest points of the ridge, a short distance from him. Had he gone to this high point [Weir Point] he would have understood the magnitude of his undertaking, and it is probable that his plan of battle would have been changed. We have no evidence that he did not go there. He could see, however, that the village was not breaking away toward the Big Horn Mountains. He must, then, have expected to find the squaws and children fleeing to the bluffs on the north, for in no other way do I account for his wide detour to the right. He must have counted upon Reno's success, and fully expected the "scatteration" of the non-combatants with the pony

---

[7] George H. Faribault (1826–1890) was Superintendent of Farming Operations And Chief Of The Indian Police at Standing Rock.

herds. The probable attack upon the families and the capture of the herds were in that event counted upon to strike consternation in the hearts of the warriors, and were elements for success upon which General Custer fully counted in the event of a daylight attack.

When Reno's advance was checked, and his left began to fall back, Chief Gall started with some of his warriors to cut off Reno's retreat to the bluffs. On his way he was excitedly hailed by "Iron Cedar," one of his warriors, who was on the high point, to hurry to him, that more soldiers were coming. This was the first intimation the Indians had of Custer's column; up to the time of this incident they had supposed that all the troops were in at Reno's attack. Custer had then crossed the valley of the dry creek, and was marching along and well up the slope of the bluff forming the second ridge back from the river, and nearly parallel to it. The command was marching rapidly in column of fours, and there was some confusion in the ranks, due probably to the unmanageableness of some excited horses.

The accepted theory for many years after the battle, and still persisted in by some writers, was that Custer's column had turned the high bluffs near the river, moved down the dry (Reno's) creek, and attempted to ford the river near the lowest point of these bluffs; that he was there met by an overpowering force and driven back; that he then divided his battalion, moved down the river with the view of attacking the village, but met with such resistance from the enemy posted along the river bank and ravines that he was compelled to fall back, fighting, to the position on the ridge. The numerous bodies found scattered between the river and ridge were supposed to be the first victims of the fight. I am now satisfied that these were men who either survived those on the ridge or attempted to escape the massacre.

Custer's route was as indicated on the map, and his column was never nearer the river or village than his final position on the ridge. The wife of Spotted Horn Bull, when giving me her account of the battle, persisted in saying that Custer's column did not attempt to cross at the ford, and appealed to her husband, who supported her statement.[8]

On the battlefield, in 1886, Chief Gall indicated Custer's route to me, and it then flashed upon me that I myself had seen Custer's trail. On June 28, while we were burying the dead, I asked Major Reno's permission to go on the high ridge east or back of the field to look for tracks of shod horses to ascertain if some of the command might not have escaped. When I reached the ridge I saw this trail, and wondered who could have made it, but dismissed the thought that it had been made by Custer's column, because it did not accord with the theory with which we were then filled, that Custer had attempted to cross at the ford, and this trail was too far back, and showed no indication of leading toward the ford. Trumpeter Penwell was my orderly and accompanied me. It was a singular coincidence that in 1886 Penwell was stationed at Fort Custer, and was my orderly when visiting the battlefield. Penwell corroborated my recollection of the trail the ford theory arose from the fact that we found there numerous tracks of shod horses, but they evidently had been made after the Indians had possessed themselves of the cavalry horses, for they rode them after capturing them. No bodies of men or horses were found anywhere near the ford, and these facts are conclusive to my mind that Custer did not go to the ford with any body of men.

As soon as Gall had personally confirmed Iron Cedar's report he sent word to the warriors battling against Reno, and to the people in the village. The greatest consternation prevailed among the families, and orders were given for them to leave at once. Before they could do so the great body of warriors had left Reno, and hastened to attack Custer. This explains why Reno was not pushed when so much confusion at the river crossing gave the Indians every opportunity of annihilating his command. Not long after the Indians began to show a strong force in Custer's front, Custer turned his

---

[8] Historian John Gray believed, based on time and motion analysis and testimony from the scout Curley, that the movement to the mouth of Medicine Tail Coulee was a feint by two companies under Captain Yates, never intending to ford there. Custer during this time took the other companies up onto what is now called Nye-Cartwright Ridge, then rejoining Yates higher up. Archaeology confirms very little firing at the mouth of Medicine Tail Coulee (Gray, *Custer's Last Campaign*, 1991).

column to the left, and advanced in the direction of the village to near a place now marked as a spring, halted at the junction of the ravines just below it, and dismounted two troops, Keogh's and Calhoun's, to fight on foot. These two troops advanced at double-time to a knoll, now marked by Crittenden's monument. The other three troops, mounted, followed them a short distance in their rear. The led horses remained where the troops dismounted. When Keogh and Calhoun got to the knoll the other troops marched rapidly to the right; Smith's troop deployed as skirmishers, mounted, and took position on a ridge, which, on Smith's left, ended in Keogh's position (now marked by Crittenden's monument), and, on Smith's right, ended at the hill on which Custer took position with Yates and Tom Custer's troops, now known as Custer's Hill, and marked by the monument erected to the command. Smith's skirmishers, holding their gray horses, remained in groups of fours.

The line occupied by Custer's battalion was the first considerable ridge back from the river, the nearest point being about half a mile from it. His front was extended about three fourths of a mile. The whole village was in full view. A few hundred yards from his line was another but lower ridge, the further slope of which was not commanded by his line. It was here that the Indians under Crazy Horse from the lower part of the village, among whom were the Cheyennes, formed for the charge on Custer's Hill. All Indians had now left Reno. Gall collected his warriors, and moved up a ravine south of Keogh and Calhoun. As they were turning this flank they discovered the led horses without any other guard than the horse-holders. They opened fire upon the horse-holders, and used the usual devices to stampede the horses—that is, yelling, waving blankets, etc.; in this they succeeded very soon, and the horses were caught up by the squaws. In this disaster Keogh and Calhoun probably lost their reserve ammunition, which was carried in the saddle-bags. Gall's warriors now moved to the foot of the knoll held by Calhoun. A large force dismounted and advanced up the slope far enough to be able to see the soldiers when standing erect, but were protected when squatting or lying down. By jumping up and firing quickly, they exposed themselves only for an instant, but drew the fire of the soldiers, causing a waste of ammunition. In the meantime

Gall was massing his mounted warriors under the protection of the slope. When everything was in readiness, at a signal from Gall the dismounted warriors rose, fired, and every Indian gave voice to the war-whoop; the mounted Indians put whip to their ponies, and the whole mass rushed upon and crushed Calhoun. The maddened mass of Indians was carried forward by its own momentum over Calhoun and Crittenden down into the depression where Keogh was, with over thirty men, and all was over on that part of the field.

In the meantime the same tactics were being pursued and executed around Custer's Hill. The warriors, under the leadership of Crow King, Crazy Horse, White Bull, "Hump," and others, moved up the ravine west of Custer's Hill, and concentrated under the shelter of the ridges on his right flank and back of his position. Gall's bloody work was finished before the annihilation of Custer was accomplished, and his victorious warriors hurried forward to the hot encounter then going on, and the frightful massacre was completed.

Smith's men had disappeared from the ridge, but not without leaving enough dead bodies to mark their line. About twenty-eight bodies of men belonging to this troop and other organizations were found in one ravine nearer the river. Many corpses were found scattered over the field between Custer's line of defense, the river, and in the direction of Reno's Hill. These, doubtless, were of men who had attempted to escape; some of them may have been sent as couriers by Custer. One of the first bodies I recognized and one of the nearest to the ford was that of Sergeant Butler of Tom Custer's troop. Sergeant Butler was a soldier of many years' experience and of known courage. The indications were that he had sold his life dearly, for near and under him were found many empty cartridge-shells.

All the Indian accounts that I know of agree that there was no organized close-quarters fighting, except on the two flanks; that with the annihilation at Custer's Hill the battle was virtually over. It does not appear that the Indians made any advance to the attack from the direction of the river; they did have a defensive force along the river and in the ravines which destroyed those who left Custer's line.

There was a great deal of firing going on over the field after the battle by the young men and boys riding about and shooting into the dead bodies.

Tuesday morning, June 27, we had reveille without the "morning guns," enjoyed the pleasure of a square meal, and had our stock properly cared for. Our commanding officer seemed to think the Indians had some "trap" set for us, and required our men to hold themselves in readiness to occupy the pits at a moment's notice. Nothing seemed determined except to stay where we were. Not an Indian was in sight, but a few pontes were seen grazing down in the valley.

About 9.30 a. m. a cloud of dust was observed several miles down the river. The assembly was sounded, the horses were placed in a protected situation, and camp-kettles and canteens were filled with water. An hour of suspense followed; but from the slow advance we concluded that they were our own troops. "But whose command is it?" We looked in vain for a gray-horse troop. It could not be Custer; it must then be Crook, for if it was Terry, Custer would be with him. Cheer after cheer was given for Crook. A white man, Harris, I think, soon came up with a note from General Terry, addressed to General Custer, dated June 26, stating that two of our Crow scouts had given information that our column had been whipped and nearly all had been killed; that he did not believe their story, but was coming with medical assistance. The scout said that he could not get to our lines the night before, as the Indians were on the alert. Very soon after this Lieutenant Bradley, 7th Infantry, came into our lines, and asked where I was. Greeting most cordially my old friend, I immediately asked, "Where is Custer?" He replied, "I don't know, but I suppose he was killed, as we counted 197 dead bodies. I don't suppose any escaped."

We were simply dumfounded. This was the first intimation we had of his fate.

It was hard to realize; it did seem impossible.

General Terry and staff, and officers of General Gibbon's column soon after approached, and their coming was greeted with

116

prolonged, hearty cheers. The grave countenance of the General awed the men to silence. The officers assembled to meet their guests.

There was scarcely a dry eye; hardly a word was spoken, but quivering lips and hearty grasping of hands gave token of thankfulness for the relief and grief for the misfortune.

During the rest of that day we were busy collecting our effects and destroying surplus property. The wounded were cared for and taken to the camp of our new friends of the Montana column. Among the wounded was saddler "Mike" Madden of my troop, whom I promoted to be sergeant, on the field, for gallantry. Madden was very fond of his grog. His long abstinence had given him a famous thirst. It was necessary to amputate his leg, which was done without administering any anesthetic; but after the amputation the surgeon gave him a good, stiff drink of brandy. Madden eagerly gulped it down, and his eyes fairly danced as he smacked his lips and said, "M-eh, doctor, cut off my other leg."

On the morning of the 28th we left our intrenchments to bury the dead of Custer's command. The morning was bright, and from the high bluffs we had a clear view of Custer's battlefield. We saw a large number of objects that looked like white boulders scattered over the field. Glasses were brought into requisition, and it was announced that these objects were the dead bodies. Captain Weir exclaimed, "Oh, how white they look!"

All the bodies, except a few, were stripped of their clothing. According to my recollection nearly all were scalped or mutilated, but there was one notable exception, that of General Custer, whose face and expression were natural; he had been shot in the temple and in the left side. Many faces had a pained, almost terrified expression. It is said that "Rain-in-the-face," a Sioux warrior, has gloried that he had cut out and had eaten the heart and liver of one of the officers.[9] Other bodies were mutilated in a disgusting manner. The bodies of Dr. Lord and Lieutenants Porter, Harrington, and Sturgis were not found, at least not recognized. The clothing of

---

[9] Unlikely and Rain-in-the-Face said it was not true.

Porter and Sturgis was found in the village, and showed that they had been killed. We buried, according to my memoranda, 212 bodies. The killed of the entire command was 265, and of wounded we had 52.

The question has been often asked, "What were the causes of Custer's defeat?" I should say:

First. The overpowering numbers of the enemy and their unexpected cohesion.

Second. Reno's panic rout from the valley.

Third. The defective extraction of the empty cartridge-shells from the carbines.

Of the first, I will say that we had nothing conclusive on which to base calculations of the numbers—and to this day it seems almost incredible that such great numbers of Indians should have left the agencies, to combine against the troops, without information relating thereto having been communicated to the commanders of troops in the field, further than that heretofore mentioned.

The second has been mentioned incidentally. The Indians say if Reno's position in the valley had been held, they would have been compelled to divide their strength for the different attacks, which would have caused confusion and apprehension, and prevented the concentration of every able-bodied warrior upon the battalion under Custer; that, at the time of the discovery of Custer's advance to attack, the chiefs gave orders for the village to move, to break up; that, at the time of Reno's retreat, this order was being carried out, but as soon as Reno's retreat was assured the order was countermanded, and the squaws were compelled to return with the pony herds; that the order would not have been countermanded had Reno's forces remained fighting in the bottom. Custer's attack did not begin until after Reno had reached the bluffs.

Of the third we can only judge by our own experience. When cartridges were dirty and corroded the ejectors did not always extract the empty shells from the chambers, and the men were compelled to use knives to get them out. When the shells were clean no great difficulty was experienced. To what extent this was a factor in causing the disaster we have no means of knowing.

A battle was unavoidable. Every man in Terry's and Custer's commands expected a battle; it was for that purpose, to punish the Indians, that the command was sent out, and with that determination Custer made his preparations. Had Custer continued his march southward—that is, left the Indian trail—the Indians would have known of our movement on the 25th, and a battle would have been fought very near the same field on which Crook had been attacked and forced back only a week before; the Indians never would have remained in camp and allowed a concentration of the several columns to attack them. If they had escaped without punishment or battle Custer would undoubtedly have been blamed.

E. S. Godfrey,
Captain 7th Cavalry.

DISCOVER MORE LOST HISTORY AT BIG BYTE BOOKS

Printed in the USA
CPSIA information can be obtained
at www.ICGtesting.com
LVHW042145200724
786078LV00005B/264

9 781519 036322